OPE

MT. ELBRUS
18,510 FEET
JUNE 2006

ASIA

MT. EVEREST
29,029 FEET
MAY 2010

CA

CARSTENSZ PYRAMID
16,023 FEET
SEPT. 2008

MT. KILIMANJARO
19,340 FEET
FEB. 2002

OCEANIA

ARCTICA

# Steps to the
# SUMMIT

## Reaching the Top
## in Business and Life

# BY PAUL FEJTEK
## with Cindy Bertram

Peak Publishing, Newport Beach, CA

To order additional copies or to get the enhanced eBook version visit:
http://StepsToTheSummit.com

FIRST EDITION, Second printing 2013

*Printed in the United States of America.*

ISBN: 978-0-9840125-1-0

Library of Congress Control Number: 2011941203

# WARNING—DISCLAIMER

Mountaineering is a dangerous activity with inherent risks. The author and Peak Publishing shall have neither liability nor responsibility to any person with respect to any loss, damage, or injury caused, or alleged to have been caused, directly or indirectly by the information contained in this book. <u>However,</u> the author is happy to accept credit for any success, or life or business improvements that may come as a result of the advice and "Steps" contained in this book. In reality, it is the reader who must take full responsibility for choosing to act upon the information presented, and therefore be prepared to embrace any and all transformational life changes it may bring.

# TABLE OF CONTENTS

# GLOSSARY OF CLIMBING
# AND OTHER TERMS

**Ascender:** A handheld mechanical safety device that slides freely up a rope as a climber ascends, but grips in the case of a fall or when downward pressure is applied. The ascender is attached to the climber's harness by a 2 to 3 foot section of rope.

**Avalanche Transceiver** (or Beacon): An electronic device that transmits a signal alerting rescuers to the location of an individual buried by an avalanche. The device also receives a signal serving a dual purpose as a search tool.

**Belay:** A technique for securing a climbing partner during an ascent using a rope and a fixed object as an anchor. The stationary partner feeds or pulls rope as the other partner climbs, minimizing the distance of a fall.

**Bergschrund:** A crevasse that forms at the upper end of a glacier when the moving ice pulls away from the slope above.

**BPI:** Brachial Plexus Injury—Full or partial paralysis of the arm and hand resulting from tearing of the complex set of nerves known as the brachial plexus. A preventable injury commonly sustained at birth (Obstetrical Brachial Plexus Injury) that can also occur as a result of traumatic injury, most frequently a motorcycle accident. *See also discussion Step 3.*

**Cache:** A supply of food, fuel, gear, or oxygen stored on the mountain (usually buried in the snow) to be retrieved and used later.

**Carabiner:** An oval shaped device made of lightweight but strong metal with a spring-loaded gate, used to attach a climber to a rope and for a variety of safety purposes.

**Cerebral Edema** (High-Altitude Cerebral Edema, or HACE): A severe, life-threatening form of altitude sickness characterized by swelling of the brain due to leakage of fluids from the capillaries. Symptoms can include headache, loss of coordination, hallucinations, loss of memory and confused irrational behavior. Can be temporarily treated with Dexamethasone, but immediate descent to a lower altitude is required.

**Chorten:** Tibetan term for a mound-like shrine containing Buddhist relics and used as a place of worship. Similar to a Stupa.

**Crampons:** Metal spikes that attach to the soles of boots enabling hiking and climbing on hard snow and ice. Modern crampons usually have 12 sharp points with two pointing forward at the toe allowing climbers to ascend a near vertical slope using a technique known as "front-pointing."

**Crevasse:** A crack or fissure in the surface of a glacier that can be wider than the length of four aluminum ladders strung end to end, and which can be up to several hundred feet deep. Crevasses are formed when a glacier flows over steep or uneven ground.

**Dexamethasone:** An anti-inflammatory steroid and immunosuppressant found to be temporarily effective in the treatment of serious high-altitude illnesses. Also known as "Dex" and typically administered by syringe in emergency situations.

**Figure 8:** A metal device shaped like the number 8 which causes friction when the rope is wrapped through. Primarily used for rappelling and sometimes for belaying.

**Fixed Line:** A rope secured to the mountain for safety purposes (usually by bolts or ice screws) to which climbers attach, using an ascender and/ or carabiner.

**Gamow Bag:** A portable pressure chamber operated by a foot pump and used to treat victims of pulmonary or cerebral edema by artificially simulating the increased air pressure of a lower altitude.

**Hoarfrost:** A deposit of needle-like ice crystals formed on the ground or on objects as a result of direct condensation at temperatures below the freezing point.

**Ice Axe:** A critical tool for a mountaineer, serving a wide variety of purposes including self-arrest of a fall, a belay anchor, stability and safety while climbing, and other uses. The head features a sharp pick on one end and an adze on the other.

**Jumar:** Also known as an Ascender—*see definition.*

**Kata:** Silk scarf, usually adorned with eight auspicious symbols, that Buddhists place around the neck of a dignitary or a loved one as a sign of respect and to wish them luck as they begin a journey or new endeavor.

**Lama:** A Tibetan high priest or spiritual master.

**Parhelion:** Bright spots on either side of the sun or a luminous ring or halo caused by diffraction of light by ice crystals in the atmosphere.

**Puja:** A Sherpa ceremony in which homage is paid and offerings made to the mountain deity. Typically performed at base camp at the beginning of an expedition.

**Pulmonary Edema** (High-Altitude Pulmonary Edema, or HAPE): A life-threatening form of altitude sickness in which fluid seeps into the lungs. Symptoms include shortness of breath while at rest, fatigue, a crackling or wheezing sound while breathing, and coughing (sometimes with blood). Can be temporarily treated with Dexamethasone and with bottled oxygen, but immediate descent to a lower altitude is required.

**Pulse Oximeter:** A medical diagnostic tool used for measuring blood oxygen saturation levels noninvasively through the skin. These small devices typically take measurements from the fingertip and also display pulse rate.

**Safety line:** A short 2 to 3 foot section of rope attached to the climbing harness on one end and to a fixed line (via a carabiner) on the other. Typically used in conjunction with an ascender as a second measure of protection.

**Serac:** A large block or column of ice found among crevasses in a glacier or icefall. Notoriously dangerous due to their propensity to collapse without warning.

**Sherpa:** An ethnic group of Tibetan descent living in the high mountains of the Eastern Himalayas. Traditionally of Buddhist belief, these strong, hard-working, and cheerful people have become a vital resource for climbers on Everest and other big Himalayan mountains. The term "Sherpa" references members of an ethnic group and is not synonymous with the term "porter." Family or last names are not commonly used in this culture and the term "Sherpa" is used instead, as in Tenzing Norgay Sherpa.

**Sirdar:** The head Sherpa organizing an expedition or trek.

**Snow Blindness:** Damage to the cornea caused by unprotected exposure to the sun's ultraviolet rays reflecting off of the snow. A painful condition causing temporary blindness.

**Stupa:** Sanskrit for "pile", a mound-like structure containing Buddhist relics and used as a place of worship. Chorten is the Tibetan word for a similar type of shrine.

**Yak:** A large, long-haired bovine found throughout the Himalayan region and Tibetan Plateau. Predominantly used by the Sherpa people as a pack animal for carrying heavy loads, but also utilized as a source for milk, cheese, clothing, and meat.

# INTRODUCTION

The bodies of more than 200 climbers remain strewn across the upper slopes of Mt. Everest. Fierce snowstorms, bone chilling winds, and powerful avalanches are all obstacles that can prevent you from reaching the top—and even kill you if you're not careful. Without question we all have our own challenges in life. Although most are not life threatening, they can just as easily kill your dreams and chances of realizing true success, if we let them.

I was presented with a difficult challenge early in my life. During birth, the nerves connecting my right arm to my spine were torn, resulting in partial paralysis. I couldn't tie my shoes, button a shirt, or shift gears in a car with my right hand. But I figured out a way to do these things, just as I figured out how to reach the top of Mt. Everest and all of the Seven Summits.

Whatever obstacles you face, whether they are physical in nature or perhaps psychological barriers; choosing how to overcome them is the primary factor determining how high you will go. To assist you in reaching new heights of success in business and life, I would like to share with you 15 specific steps that helped me overcome significant adversities and accomplish a multitude of important personal and professional goals. These Steps are presented alongside the chronicles of my adventures climbing the Seven Summits. At the end of each chapter you will find a Step relevant to the story, with insights into how that Step will guide you to success. Collectively these Steps will create a clear and proven path to elevate you towards reaching your own summit. If you're ready for an adventure, come join me on the journey, and enjoy the climb!

*To Denise: my wife, my climbing partner, and my best friend.*
*Your unwavering love and support makes life the greatest adventure.*

# Steps to the
# SUMMIT

## Reaching the Top
## in Business and Life

# PROLOGUE

The distinctive and commanding beat of the helicopter rotors rivaled the beating of my heart as we touched down on a precariously small perch. I had waited days for the cloud cover of the storm to break, making it safe to fly. Tim abruptly slid open the door of the big Bell Ranger and we hopped out and took quick cover from the veritable blizzard created as the helicopter powerfully lifted off the snow-crested peak. We watched as the chopper banked and dove back down the mountain, eventually disappearing from sight and sound. We were left alone in a calm silence on the mountaintop. It was a magical winter day in the pristine and isolated Monashee range of the Canadian Rockies. The natural alpine beauty of spectacular snow-covered peaks surrounded us, and there were no other people as far as the eye could see. The air was cold and crisp, and it filled my nostrils and lungs as I took a deep breath preparing for what I was about to do. It was a perfect day, in fact the perfect moment, to kneel down on one knee in the deep snow and ask my girlfriend to be my wife.

Denise and I met in high school, measuring angles and circumferences in Mrs. Frost's Geometry class. I didn't have the nerve to ask her out on a date until four years later while attending college at the University of Southern California. She said yes to the date and she said yes when I proposed on one knee on top of that remote peak in British Columbia. With a shiny new ring on her finger and wearing an avalanche transceiver for safety, we began carving turns down the mountain through fresh powder. It was our very first time helicopter skiing and the sensation of freely floating and turning through the feathery untouched snow was invigorating.

I had been a part-time ski instructor in Big Bear, a local Southern California mountain resort, for the past seven years. What had started as a fun college job turned into a passion, so after graduation I continued to work on weekends and holidays. I taught Denise how to ski and she picked it up quickly, also joining the ski school staff the very next season. It was on those slopes that our love for the mountains grew, along with our love for each other. Looking back to that day when I first saw Denise in Geometry class, it seems quite appropriate that the Greek definition of geometry is literally "earth measurement." We would soon find ourselves going to great measures to make our way to the farthest and highest points around the globe.

> *"Love does not consist in gazing at each other, but in looking outward together in the same direction."*
> *—Antoine de Saint-Exupery*

Neither of us knew at that time, while heli-skiing and carving turns through the powder, exactly where those turns would lead us through our life together as husband and wife. We didn't know we would find ourselves in South America staring up at a massive boulder as it tumbled down toward us, out of control, hitting a member of our climbing party. Or what it would be like to remove a glove, soaked red with blood from my right arm. We couldn't have imagined the tragic death of our guide, killed by an avalanche, or the need to complete Body Disposal and Repatriation forms for one another. And we didn't know we would witness the body of a man being carried through our camp after dying in his wife's arms on the mountain.

No, at the moment when Denise accepted my marriage proposal high up on that mountain in British Columbia, all I knew for certain was that I just closed the deal of a lifetime!

# DREAM BIG AND STEP UP

*Allow yourself to dream big and let your imagination run wild.
Taking that first step will build confidence and reinforce
a critical pattern of success.*

## AFRICA CALLING

When Denise and I exchanged our vows, we compiled a list of goals for our life together. Aside from the always-important aspirations of love, happiness and solid communication, high on our list was travel. A short three years later, while building our marital partnership, and stocking up on vacation days, a pivotal email arrived from one of Denise's longtime friends. She had pursued her own dream and was living in Africa as a Peace Corps volunteer. An invitation to come for a visit was extended and we quickly accepted.

It was as if the timing had been designed for us and a unique opportunity for a big adventure had been placed in our laps. At what other time in our lives would we get the chance to stay in a remote African village, where so few foreigners ever venture? Africa is one of those continents many only dream of visiting. A place of serene beauty with a unique combination of expansive plains and exotic animals; it is also home to the largest freestanding volcano in the world—the glacial capped Mt.

> *"Whatever you can do, or dream you can do, begin it. Boldness has genius, power and magic in it."*
> —Goethe

Kilimanjaro. This would be a prime opportunity to check off one goal from our destination dream list.

I previously read the book "Seven Summits" by Dick Bass and knew all about this 19,340-foot snow-capped volcano emerging high above the African flatlands in Tanzania. So in addition to the requisite African safari, and visiting our friends, we could not resist the allure of climbing Mt. Kilimanjaro. What I didn't know was that this decision would set into motion an exhilarating eight year quest to do what only 65 people in the world at that time had ever done before: climb the highest peaks on each of the earth's seven continents.

Surely we weren't qualified to be members of this exclusive club of elite mountaineers. True, I had picked up a few outdoor skills as a kid in the Boy Scouts on my path to becoming an Eagle Scout. But seriously, all of the Seven Summits including Mt. Everest? No way! Undaunted and perhaps blissfully unaware of the challenges we would face, we began a monumental journey when we took our first step up the slopes of this giant African mountain.

One of the unique aspects of climbing Kilimanjaro is passing through five distinct climatic zones en route to the summit. Each day began with a five to six hour hike and ended at a progressively higher camp. We started out in the Bushland, where most of the mountain villages are located. Being the "prepared" Boy Scout, I was proud of my hi-tech water filter, which was quickly rendered useless. Apparently it was not designed to handle the heavy sediment, nor the frogs and worms that inundated the small river. Our gastro-intestinal systems were not designed to handle the water either, with or without these critters. As a result we all ended up getting dysentery. I learned a lesson the hard way that it would have been a better choice to use iodine tablets to treat the contaminated water.

I learned another valuable lesson from this experience as well. As a consequence of our intestinal malady, our toilet paper supply quickly diminished. We asked our guides whether or not they had some. I remember the scene vividly. Dissmus yelled over to Samson who was in another tent, posing a question in their local Swahili dialect. His response was directed toward Simon who in turn shouted something in Swahili to one of the others. Joachim chimed in and pretty soon an escalating chatter in Swahili was simultaneously going back and forth among all of our guides and porters. Denise and I looked at one another as all of this was happening, knowing full well the answer before the response eventually came back in English; "No, we don't have any toilet paper."

Along with his girlfriend Michelle, my close friend and college roommate Shawn Sedlacek had joined us for this trip, and it was a good thing we were accustomed to sharing. We only had half a roll of toilet paper remaining among us, so to this day the phrase, "only four squares apiece" still gets a laugh.

From the Bushland we continued along, and at 5,900 feet we hiked through the lush glades of the Rainforest Zone, which accumulates the highest levels of precipitation on the mountain, creating the most humid conditions of the climb. Camping here was challenging—everything was constantly wet. This time of year was supposedly the "dry season", but you wouldn't know it with all the hail, sleet and snow we encountered on our trek.

The Moorland began at 9,200 feet, and marked the transition from rainforest conditions to desert. Lush trees and ferns were replaced by shrubs, and temperatures were much lower at this level. Off went our rain ponchos and on went the layers and heavy jackets. The constant change in weather was so dramatic that it felt as if we were experiencing a different season each day.

At 13,100 feet we reached the Alpine Desert zone. The air at this elevation felt clear and dry, and the temperatures dropped below freezing at night. We not only had to continuously adapt to the extreme weather changes; our bodies were struggling to function in the increasingly thin air at this altitude. Meanwhile our dysentery issues from the bad water we drank previously persisted, depleting our systems and causing a serious risk of dehydration. Would we be able to make it? This trip was no longer just a dream vacation, but a bona fide physical challenge.

We were now at 15,200 feet and had never hiked this high before. We weren't sure whether our tired and drained bodies would hold out at even higher altitudes. We lifted our eyes, apprehensively examining the long trail above us. The path leads climbers into the aptly named Arctic

Zone. There is no vegetation or animal life in this region, and oxygen levels are half of what we were used to living at sea level.

It was day five of our ascent and now it was time for the final test, to see whether we could make it all the way to the summit. We prepared our gear, slept for a few hours, and left camp at 1:00 a.m. We knew it would be a long climb of over 4,000 vertical feet in order to reach the summit. Therefore leaving in the middle of the night would allow enough time for us to get up and back down to camp before the typical afternoon storms rolled in, a common occurrence on most big mountains.

As we began hiking the winds became fierce, like nothing we had ever experienced before. It was almost as if the mountain was taunting us, displaying her supreme force. "How dare you tiny humans take on such a big challenge as me," I imagined her warning. She threw powerful wind gusts of 80 to 90 mph our way, catching us off guard and forcing us to grab hold of large rocks along the trail to prevent from being knocked over. As the beam of my headlamp pierced the darkness I could see finely ground bits of volcanic dust whipping in front of my face. Fortunately we came prepared with ski goggles to protect our eyes from an otherwise blinding irritation.

After seven hours of hiking throughout the dark, cold, and windy night, our eyes were rewarded with a magical visual display. The winds calmed down considerably and we watched the first rays of the sun cast an orange glow upon the distinctive glacial cap of the majestic mountain we had admired so much from down below. And as we hiked along the rim of the volcano, the sun began to illuminate the massive interior of the crater.

The next thing we knew, we were taking our final steps to the 19,340-foot summit of Mt. Kilimanjaro. Despite the hardships we had put them through, our bodies performed for us, and we managed to climb far higher than we had ever been before. As we gazed across the horizon admiring this stunning vista we had only dreamed about previously, we silently set a new goal: Mt. Aconcagua, highest in South America.

*Mt. Kilimanjaro summit, February 2002*

"After climbing a great hill, one finds that there are many more hills to climb. I have taken a moment to rest, to steal a view of the glorious vista that surrounds me, to look back on the distance I have come. But I can only rest for a moment, for with freedom comes responsibilities, and I dare not linger, for my long walk has not yet ended."

—Nelson Mandela

*Step to the Summit*
## DREAM BIG AND STEP UP

Taking your first step towards an important goal in business and life can be intimidating and filled with self-doubt and reasonable justifications as to why it shouldn't be attempted. Too many of us get caught up with the enormity of the end goal and rationalize all of the possible roadblocks that might prevent us from reaching our target. However, for those few who muster the courage to dream big and forge ahead towards their own "Everest-sized" goals anyway without any guarantee of success, the rewards are great.

The secret is to carve stepping stones up towards that high goal and then instruct your brain to take that first step, no matter how small. The satisfaction we receive from accomplishing objectives that move us up to a slightly higher altitude, possesses an incredible power, giving us the confidence to go even higher next time. Repeating this pattern of achieving small but progressively larger goals burns a critical habit of success into our psyche. Before standing on the roof of Africa, we hiked to the top of Mt. Whitney, which at 14,500 feet is the highest point in the contiguous United States. And before attempting that, our boots made their way up many peaks of much lower elevations. And now, with the feeling we could go even higher still, my adventurous wife and I studied a map of the world and planned our journey to the next continent.

> *"If you want to be happy, set a goal that commands your thoughts, liberates your energy, and inspires your hopes."* —**Andrew Carnegie**

…and then lace up your boots, throw on your backpack, and hit the trail!

---
## *Step 2*
---

# LIVE COURAGEOUSLY

*Find the strength to take bold steps and remove the biggest*
*obstacle in your route to success—yourself.*

---

## THE STONE SENTINEL

After Africa, almost three years passed before we were finally able to get away to tackle South America's highest peak. At 22,843 feet Mt. Aconcagua, "The Stone Sentinel" is located in the Andes of Argentina near the border with Chile. Cerro Aconcagua is also known as the "Roof of the Americas." It is the highest mountain in South America, and also the highest peak in the world outside of Asia. It is the second highest of the Seven Summits, next to Mt. Everest. In January of 2005, we boarded a 12-hour flight to Mendoza, Argentina, not yet realizing that this 15-day expedition would not only be a physical test of endurance but also an extreme test of our courage.

On day three of our adventure we hiked into Plaza de Mulas Base Camp at 14,000 feet. It is here that we learned about a Brazilian husband and wife team that had suffered a harrowing fate. Eduardo Silva and his wife had reached the summit well after what could be considered a safe turn-around time, and they were caught in a storm on the way back down. Although his wife survived, Eduardo gasped his last breath and perished in her arms on the trail. He had suffered from high-altitude pulmonary edema (HAPE), in which the lungs fill with fluid due to a shortage of oxygen. It wasn't until several days later before they could retrieve his body, and so it was that we witnessed it being carried through our Base Camp. This was truly a sobering reminder of the dangers involved in what we were attempting. Aconcagua would be by far the highest altitude we had ever attempted. After this incident the question then became, would any reasonable person have blamed us if we chose to call it quits at that point? After all, we were also a husband and wife climbing team, and we didn't have anywhere near the climbing experience that the Silvas had.

As if that weren't enough to rattle us, we also witnessed a massive avalanche on the South Face, luckily from a safe distance away. In a separate incident, a huge boulder came tumbling down toward our group and to get out of its path we all scrambled like cockroaches when the kitchen light is turned on. Sandra, one of the members of our team, wasn't fast enough and was hit in the leg by the boulder. She was shaken and bruised but fortunately able to walk away. Still, the harsh reality of what we had signed up for was staring us in the face, and its voice was loud and clear.

> *"Courage is resistance to fear, mastery of fear—not absence of fear."*
> —*Mark Twain*

We spent that first week carefully acclimatizing, doing "carries" from Base Camp to the higher camps. This not only gets some of your gear to the next camp while lightening the load in the process, but it also helps to prepare your body for the higher elevation. The adjustment period takes time, and not all people react the same to altitude. In fact, three of the climbers in our party had to be evacuated by helicopter due to extremely low blood oxygen saturation levels. This is a strong indicator of HAPE (as Eduardo Silva had suffered). We said goodbye to our climbing partners as they boarded the chopper to a lower elevation. Fortunately, our bodies seemed to have adapted more quickly than the others and that confidence gave us the courage to continue on. We now worked our way toward the attainable goal of reaching the top.

After nearly two weeks on the mountain, we were finally in position at Camp 3 known as White Rocks at 19,100 feet. At 3:00 a.m. we awoke to a star-filled sky—perfect for a summit attempt. The only drawback to having completely clear skies, is that temperatures are much colder. Cloud cover acts as an insulating layer, trapping the thermal radiation from the earth. We began climbing at the coldest part of the night, desperately hoping the warming rays of the sun would soon appear. It was well below zero degrees Fahrenheit and Denise's fingers became increasingly cold with each passing hour. Eventually, at nearly 21,000 feet we reached the Refugio Independencia, a dilapidated wooden emergency shelter which hardly seemed fit for its intended purpose. We needed to make a decision concerning what to do about Denise's cold hands. If we couldn't warm them up we would need to turn around and go back down.

Meanwhile two brothers from Spain who were part of our group, were struggling. The altitude was too much for them and they decided they had reached their limit. In addition to the three who were evacuated by helicopter earlier, our group was shrinking fast. "Should we go back as well?" we thought. We had already witnessed another tragedy on this mountain with Eduardo Silva and his wife.

Denise removed her gloves and tucked her hands inside my jacket and underneath my armpits in an effort to warm her fingers. This seemed to do the trick and after a while, we felt comfortable in continuing onward and upward.

It had been a total of 13 long hours since we left Camp 3, and with a considerable physical effort made in the thin air of this extremely high altitude, we finally reached the summit. It was an incredible feeling of elation and satisfaction, to confront our challenges and fears, and reach our goal.

*Mt. Aconcagua summit, January 2005 – 22,843 feet*

# FROM RUSSIA WITH LOVE

Less than a year and a half later, we climbed Mt. Elbrus, the highest peak on the European continent. Elbrus is located in the Caucasus Mountains of Russia. Its summit stands at 18,510 feet. Although it doesn't resemble one, Elbrus is actually an inactive volcano. Its annual death toll is among the highest of the Seven Summits, often due to unprepared climbers who underestimate its sometimes harsh conditions. In fact, eleven climbers from a Russian and Ukrainian team died high up on the mountain just two weeks before we arrived, and they were still searching for the bodies of four of the climbers while we were there. This was yet another test of our faith and courage to get to the top.

Russia was unlike any other trip we had taken. The entire operation seemed a little sketchy to us. At times I felt like we'd made a deal with the Russian mafia to be allowed on their mountain. Everything was done in cash; the night before our first climbing day, Denise and I counted out over two thousand U.S. dollars in small bills to the chain-smoking guiding service representative on the bed in our dimly lit hotel room. I had visions of the door busting open and Russian police charging through the thick smoke. The oddities didn't stop there. Our climbing guide Oksana was much like a drill sergeant; her heavy accent and harsh authoritative manner were ironically befitting of a bygone Soviet era found only in the movies. I'm not sure if it was courage or simply the fear of Oksana that propelled us up the mountain.

We had other things to be fearful of on this mountain as well. It seemed to us the safety standards were severely lacking. Perhaps it was a cultural difference but the Russians just didn't appear to value life as much as we do. Case in point, I learned that Oksana was not carrying a rope on our summit day. Any mountain guide in the U.S. or most other parts of the world, would be carrying a rope just as routinely as a doctor would have his stethoscope. Luckily we didn't have any emergency situations that would have necessitated use of this basic tool of the trade. We did make it to the peak of Mt. Elbrus, the third of our Seven Summits, and most importantly we got back down safely.

*Mt. Elbrus, June 2006 – 18,510 feet*

# DANGER ON DENALI

In June of 2007, Mt. McKinley in Alaska was next. Mt. McKinley is also known by its Native American name Denali, meaning "The Great One." It is the highest peak in North America at 20,320 feet. Due to its latitudinal location near the Arctic Circle and its proximity to the Bering Sea, Denali is characterized by extreme cold temperatures reaching minus 75 degrees and blustery, long-lasting snowstorms.

We came fully equipped for this one—crampons, ice axes, plenty of rope, cold weather gear and loads of courage. And we needed all of it—especially the courage. This was particularly true after witnessing what happened to a German climber named Stefan high up on the mountain, on a dangerous traverse known as (ironically enough) the "Autobahn." This section of the climbing route, located above high camp at 17,000 feet, gained its name many years ago in an irreverent manner after several German climbers fell to their deaths, rapidly accelerating to great speeds while careening down the steep, icy slope. There is another section of the mountain similarly named in questionable taste, after several Japanese climbers died by this same means, and is now known as the "Orient Express."

*The "Autobahn", Mt. McKinley*

The situation with Stefan was slightly different, but equally as frightening. We were preparing to make our summit attempt from high camp, when radio chatter on the emergency channel broke out. We looked up at the Autobahn and noticed a long line of climbers back-logged along this expansive and steep terrain. Apparently Stefan had become dizzy and passed out at an inopportune place. Fortunately he was roped in for safety and didn't slide to his demise. But his team could not revive him and get him mobile again. Eventually they administered an emergency injection of the anti-inflammatory steroid dexamethasone or "Dex" as it is known, which helped Stefan regain consciousness and his chances for survival. The guides from our team scrambled to assist in what luckily ended up being a successful rescue effort.

I recalled my conversation with Stefan a few days prior to the incident down at the 14,000 foot camp where many teams were spending time waiting for the weather to improve. Stefan told me he was an architect working on a big building project back home in Germany. He joked that his company was concerned something could happen to him while climbing Denali so they decided to take out a key man life insurance policy on him. He thought it was a waste of money but was flattered they thought so highly of him. It made me think, here I was a Managing Director at my investment banking firm but nobody placed a key man life insurance policy on me! Should I be more concerned about what could happen high up on Denali? After seeing what happened to Stefan, the potential for disaster seemed even more evident.

Our planned departure for the summit was delayed by a day due to the situation with Stefan; nonetheless the weather cooperated with us just a bit longer. We felt quite strong and performed well high up on the mountain. We crossed the Autobahn safely and eventually made our way along the narrow, wind-swept corniced summit ridge all the way to the highest point in North America.

*Mt. McKinley summit ridge, June 2007*

Skilled mountaineers will always tell you, "Reaching the summit is only half the battle. You have to make it back down safely." This is particularly true on Denali. It is a notoriously dangerous mountain due largely to the deep crevasses that riddle the Kahiltna Glacier at lower elevations. Many climbers have met their maker by falling into these fissures in the glacier which can be several hundred and in some cases up to 1,000 feet deep. For this reason climbers travel roped together in teams of three or four to arrest the fall should their partner punch through a thin layer of snow concealing a crevasse.

I led our rope team on the way back down. Denise was tied in directly behind me as we descended to the lower slopes of the mountain with a sense of satisfaction at our accomplishment. It was a stunningly beautiful day. We watched the late afternoon sky turn from yellow to a radiant orange as we hiked down the mountain. Suddenly the snow beneath me collapsed, and WHAM I plunged into a crevasse! Denise quickly secured the rope, and I kicked my crampons into the wall of the crevasse to prevent slipping further down. As I did, the snow that was packed around my body fell away, revealing the depth of the icy, dark blue belly of the beast beneath me. At that moment I flashed to the Brazilian couple on Aconcagua and thought about Eduardo slipping away from his wife as he greeted death. This was not going to happen to Denise and me.

I carefully maneuvered out of the crevasse, and climbed up to the edge to safety. It wasn't until later when we had finished our descent for the day and were resting in our tent that I recounted the moment of fear that I felt when I was faced with the possibility of never being with my wife again. I told Denise how much I loved her and how much she meant to me. She expressed the same and told me how helpless and frustrated she felt watching as I clung desperately to the edge of that crevasse. Denise then tried to lighten the mood and joked with me that the real reason she felt so helpless and frustrated was because she wanted to take a picture of me in my precarious state, but I had the camera in my pocket!

Denali quickly taught us that stepping out of our comfort zones could be intimidating and scary, but incredibly rewarding. It also taught us that Everest was within our reach.

*Step to the Summit*
# LIVE COURAGEOUSLY

After becoming the first person to successfully climb Mt. Everest in 1953, Sir Edmund Hillary said, "It's not the mountain we conquer, but ourselves." How often do we allow *ourselves* to get in the way of doing great things? Do we make sensible-sounding excuses that are really just clever ways to conceal our fears? Or is it fear of failure, fear of rejection or criticism, and even the fear of success that gets in our way?

Have the courage to acknowledge your goals and dreams by writing them down and talking about them openly with those who support and care about you. Certainly taking that first step requires courage, and as we climb higher and start progressively realizing success, the slope can become extremely steep. We can sabotage our own success by becoming complacent, or by feeling that we are not worthy of what we have achieved or of the new level of income we have attained. At the same time we are trying to "conquer ourselves," we must have the courage to fight gravity to climb higher and resist the downward pull of others.

Just like the analogy about crabs in a bucket that try to prevent the other crabs from escaping, there will always be people who discount, discourage, and dismiss your dreams as unrealistic, foolhardy, or too risky. However, history is filled with examples of brave individuals who ignored the naysayers and went on to passionately pursue their dreams anyway. Thomas Edison, the Wright Brothers, Walt Disney, Abraham Lincoln, Mother Teresa, and Martin Luther King are just a few of the classic and well known illustrations of this type of courage in action. There are countless others making an impact in their businesses, communities and in society by living courageously.

When it comes to climbing the Seven Summits and mountaineering in general, the physical risks carry a far more severe penalty than simply the risk of failing, being criticized, or experiencing a financial loss. It takes inner strength to continue on and manage the fear and doubts that arise (particularly when a dead body is carried through your base camp).

To the critics who didn't understand or appreciate our dream to climb the Seven Summits and who felt it was "too risky," I have two comments. First, it is important to comprehend and accept the risks of any major undertaking, and then carefully manage those risks wherever possible. Second, there is an inherent risk in choosing not to dream or pursue those dreams. The result of that choice is to end up living a life of mediocrity. Quite frankly, *that* path is simply too risky!

> *"Do you want to be safe and good, or do you want to take a chance and be great?"*
> —*Jimmy Johnson*

In order to live life to the fullest I encourage you to "C.L.I.M.B." to the top! This is an acronym I created to remember that:

Courageous
Living
Improves
My
Being

The "B" is interchangeable and you will see through practice that in addition, Courageous Living Improves My Belief, which leads to improved Behavior, and as a consequence improved behavior can result in an improved Body and even an improved Bank account!

Apply these principles in your personal and professional life and you will soon stand high above the rest as a "C.L.I.M.B.E.R.":

**C**ourageous
**L**iving
**I**gnites
**M**y
**B**est
**E**ver
**R**esults!

---- *Step 3* ----

# DISCOVER YOUR CREATIVITY

*When challenges arise, tap in to the creative recesses of your*
*brain to find the tools enabling you to blaze a new trail.*

---

## WELCOME TO THE JUNGLE

When traveling to remote destinations around the world to climb mountains, you become quite accustomed to unexpected variables changing your plans. After our success on Denali, Denise and I set out to attempt our fifth summit in September of 2008. This time it was Carstensz Pyramid, the highest mountain on the Oceania continent. Located in the central highlands of the Papua province of Indonesia, "Puncak Jaya", as the local tribes people call it, stands at 16,023 feet. While it certainly was not the highest elevation we'd climbed at this point, this one was about to be the most challenging.

The Yosemite Decimal System is a set of numeric ratings describing the difficulty of hikes and climbs. The scale ranges from 1 on the low end (basic walking) to 5 (technical climbing). Further classification of the technical climbing rating spans from 5.0 to a maximum of 5.13. Anything within this range requires the protection of ropes, otherwise a fall can cause severe injury or death. Measuring in at 5.8, Carstensz Pyramid is actually the most technically challenging of the Seven Summits. Even for experienced climbers, a 5.8 is ambitious. For a climber using mainly one arm, it could very well be the biggest challenge of his life.

I was born with a condition known as a BPI, which stands for Brachial Plexus Injury. The Brachial Plexus is a complex set of nerves originating from the spinal cord and controlling all movement of the shoulder, arm and hand. In certain situations during the birth process, particularly with larger babies (I weighed over eleven pounds at birth), the shoulder can become "stuck" inside the birth canal. As a result of excessive force applied to the baby's neck and head during delivery, the brachial plexus can become stretched and torn, causing full or partial paralysis of the arm. This actually occurs at an alarmingly frequent rate. Three to four out of every 1,000 babies born in the United States are born with a BPI. In simple terms, that is one baby every hour. Brachial Plexus Injuries occur more often than Down Syndrome, Muscular Dystrophy or Spina Bifida, yet many people are unaware of the condition. It is entirely preventable through proper birthing procedures and positions, yet it still occurs four decades after changing my life forever.

Growing up with this challenge, I was forced to find solutions to simple tasks that other kids find easy, like tying shoes or buttoning a shirt. Overcoming challenges quickly became a way of life; a solution-focused mindset, if you will. And I have to give credit where credit is due—to my mother. She constantly supported and encouraged me with positive reinforcement, which I found to be very empowering. Throughout my childhood my mom enrolled me in everything she could that would help strengthen my right arm: drum lessons, swim team, judo practice—she even taught me how to water-ski. As she subjected me to one physical activity after another that required the extreme coordination and strength of my arm, I would often think to myself, "Didn't anyone tell this lady that my arm doesn't work like all of the other kids?"

Looking back, I'm sure it had to be emotionally exhausting for her to intentionally put her son in situations where time and time again, she had to watch me fall down, come in last place, or simply fail. But she instilled deeply within me the notion that, "You can do anything!" And through that, she proved to me (and I proved to myself) that anything is possible. Through trial and error, and total persistence, I *did* figure out a

> **"The chief enemy of creativity is 'good' sense."**
> —*Pablo Picasso*

way to play the drums. I *did* figure out a way to hold onto that water-ski rope. I *did* figure out a way to throw the other kids onto *their* backs in judo practice! And as an adult, I figured out a way to beat more than two out of every three able-bodied men in my age group at various competitive triathlons.

This firmly rooted notion that "I can do anything" is what helped me overcome the formidable physical and technical challenge of climbing Carstensz Pyramid with only one good arm. It was reinforced by the amazing story of Aron Ralston.

Aron Ralston is a mountain climber who gained notoriety in May 2003 while climbing through slot canyons in Utah. An accident forced him to amputate his own right arm with a dull knife in order to free himself from a fallen boulder that had crushed it. Ralston was hiking alone, and hadn't alerted anyone of his plans. Deep in the canyon, pinned against the wall, he knew that no one would be searching for him. He spent the next five days rationing what little food and water he had, at the same time struggling to free his arm. He eventually ran out of water and couldn't release his arm, so he carved his name, date of birth and death into the sandstone canyon wall and videotaped goodbyes to his family. But then he came up with an idea to save his own life. He began the incomprehensible process of amputating his own arm below the right elbow. He performed the horrific task with the only instrument he had available—a cheap multi use tool with a dull blade. Miraculously he was able to do it, and in turn free himself. He then rappelled down a 65-foot canyon wall, and hiked out into the midday sun undoubtedly in shock. Other hikers ultimately came to his aid, and then a helicopter airlifted him out of the canyon.

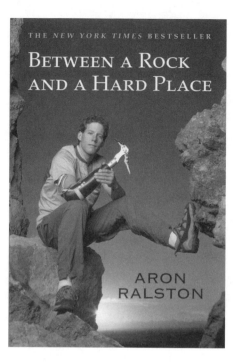

*Image courtesy of Atria Books*

Aron's remarkable story was recounted in his book "Between a Rock and a Hard Place" and later made into the acclaimed movie *127 Hours,* starring James Franco. It was the cover photo of the original book published in 2004 that caught my attention. Aron was pictured wearing a customized prosthetic arm with a sharp pointed ice axe on the end, in place of where the hand would be otherwise. After his accident this innovative device allowed Aron to return to the mountains he loved and climb once again. The loss of his arm set no limitations for Aron, he simply had to get creative. So that's what I did.

I knew the technical difficulty of Carstensz Pyramid could be a major roadblock for me in climbing the Seven Summits. So, I paid a visit to the local climbing gym to see how I would fare on the 5.8 rated sections. The brightly colored artificial rocks on these climbing walls all designate different skill levels, and for the life of me I simply could not scale the red-colored 5.8 routes. It was beyond frustrating for me, as I just did not have the gripping strength in my right hand to climb the wall. But I was not about to give up on my goal. I could hear the words of my mother playing in my head: "You can do anything!" And then I remembered the photo of Aron Ralston with his ice axe prosthetic arm. I took a trip to the local hardware store and walked up and down the aisles. It was in the coat hook section that the idea for "The Claw" climbing device was born. Using a wrist brace, a simple $3.00 coat hook and some power tools in my garage, I was able to invent my way to the top of those 5.8 routes at the climbing gym! Denise was belaying me from below and after experiencing this breakthrough success, I enthusiastically told her "Let's book some flights to Indonesia!"

> *"Creativity can solve almost any problem. The creative act, the defeat of habit by originality overcomes everything."*
> *—George Lois*

*Makeshift climbing device using hardware store coat hook*

The Carstensz Pyramid climb started out as anything but smooth. Typhoons, canceled flights, our delayed arrival and miscommunication by the local Indonesian guide service nearly cost us that fifth summit. Upon landing in Jakarta, we were stunned to learn that the rest of our group had left without us. But we didn't give up, we had trained too hard to throw in the towel. We scrambled like participants in the television show Amazing Race to get ourselves on a flight to Timika, in the Papua province, in an attempt to catch up to the group. Once there we had to charter a bush plane just for the two of us at a cost of $3,000. The plane flew us over hundreds of square miles of dense jungle to a faraway dirt landing strip near the village of Sugapa, where the rest of our group was waiting, getting ready to start the long journey to Base Camp.

For six laborious days, mud, rain, entangling tree roots and hanging vines, steep slopes and angry rivers all conspired against us to impede our progress towards Base Camp. It was a daily routine of powering ourselves up, down and through the most difficult terrain we had ever experienced. The incessant rain caused knee-high mud puddles (often infested with leeches), and lots of slipping and falling (which in turn meant lots of cuts and bruises) but it did little to dampen our spirits. We had worked too hard and had already been through so much just to get here. Despite the physical and emotional toll it was taking on me and Denise, we decided to make the most of it.

Historically, climbers have taken a more direct route to Base Camp: straight through the Freeport-McMoRan Mine—the largest gold and copper mine in the world. But there was a caveat to going this way, as the mineworkers must illegally smuggle the climbers through in the back of a truck. However, the mine owners had recently cracked down on the practice, which in turn forced us to find another means to get to Base Camp. Our local Indonesian guides had pioneered a new, much longer route from the North, passing by foot through some remote Dani and Moni tribal hunting villages. Denise and I were surprised to learn from our guides that we were only the 14th and 15th Westerners respectively, to ever follow this remote route deep into the jungle. As we watched our guides and porters wield their machetes in order to clear a path, we knew we were in a place far off the map.

A bright spot along the way was definitely the tribal people we encountered. We trekked by their villages, clusters of primitive round huts with thatched roofs. They greeted us with honest smiles and a natural curiosity. We were dressed in full hiking gear, and most of these tribesmen wore nothing but a traditional penis sheath, made from a gourd and known as a koteka. We learned that the longer the gourd, the more seniority the man has within his tribal hierarchy.

*Dani tribe members hunting for wild pigs with bow and arrow*

The Dani and Moni people spend their days hunting, and their skin was weathered with years of sun and hard living. When they smiled at us, their faces looked like handcrafted mosaics. The children gathered around our group; many of them had never seen white people before. It was quite different than some of the African villages we had visited, where outsiders are not as much of a novelty. These children (and adults) were inquisitive and innocently fascinated just to look at us, and touch our skin. And when we showed them their own images instantly captured on our digital camera, they were shocked and astonished. They must have thought we were magical spirit visitors with supernatural powers.

As recently as the 1960s, these tribal people were still practicing cannibalism, referring to humans as "long pigs." In fact, many years ago while in the region studying the tribal culture, Michael Rockefeller, a fourth generation descendant of the famed Rockefeller family, disappeared—and his body was never found. Some speculate that he was captured and eaten by the cannibalistic tribespeople. As I shook hands with the village chief I was honored to have the privilege of being a rare ambassador of the Western world, but I couldn't help but wonder if he was hungry as he assessed me from head to toe.

After the sixth arduous day, we finally dragged ourselves into Base Camp at 13,800 feet. Although we were a little bruised and battered from the march through the jungle, our culturally rich experience nourished our souls. We collapsed into our tent and tried not to think about the physically demanding return trek. We were finally able to rest for a day, but before we knew it, it was time to start out for the summit!

The alarm went off at 1:00 a.m. on Thursday, September 25, 2008. We crawled out of our warm sleeping bags, ate a quick breakfast and made a final check of our gear. We left Base Camp in total darkness to head for the summit. About an hour into the journey we hit the first of more than twenty fixed lines that would provide protection from the exposed rock faces we were about to climb. My headlamp pierced the darkness above to reveal the near vertical pitch we were expected to scale. After a careful scan for available handholds, I quickly realized "The Claw" would be necessary here and I attached it over my right glove.

*"The Claw" on Carstensz Pyramid*

Next, I clipped my self-belay device known as an ascender (or jumar) to the rope which would serve to arrest any unexpected slips or falls. Then I connected my safety line and started climbing. Higher up, some of the handholds were so few and far between that The Claw actually turned out to be a critical piece of equipment. Despite its unsophisticated manufacturing, it performed without failure. The rock was unlike anything we had ever seen before. It had a pronounced texture with sharp-edged ridges protruding as much as half an inch from the surface. This unusual rock was great for fingerholds and for The Claw, but due to its sharpness, not so great for clothing and flesh. This was a harsh lesson that my right elbow would learn a little later.

The next major obstacle to overcome was a wide "gap" spanning the ridgeline we were climbing. It was a 75 foot gaping expanse above a massive drop that would result in certain death in the case of a fall. This was the kind of barrier that would clearly prevent the faint of heart from going any farther. However we were focused on reaching our goal, and had a plan to conquer this challenge.

The "Tyrolean Traverse" is a method of crossing a large void between two high points using a rope. Remember the opening scene of the movie "Cliffhanger"? Denise and I stared at the ropes tenuously connecting the rock ledges on either side of the gap. We tightened our climbing harnesses and hoped they wouldn't fail. Our guide Poxi clipped his locking carabiner to the ice-encrusted lines left from a previous expedition. We had no way of knowing how long those ropes had been there exposed to the elements and we really didn't know whether or not they would hold. But Poxi was going, so I guessed we were going too! He began to pull himself across, hanging from the ropes as the ice dramatically broke off and fell into the chasm, eventually shattering on the sharp rocks below. Desperately trying not to focus on the depth of the ominous gorge, it was my turn to snap my carabiner onto the ropes. With a few twists it was locked into place and my fate was now affixed to the integrity of those ropes as well. Denise wished me luck and stood ready with the video camera as I leaned back and hoped for the best.

That moment when my full weight tugged against the ropes and my harness, was the critical point when something terrible could potentially occur, I thought. My heart was pounding with a powerful force and adrenaline was coursing through my veins. Fortunately the ropes held, and I pulled myself across the gap and over the ominous void below.

*Denise crossing the "gap" using the Tyrolean Traverse*

Without incident, we successfully prevailed over the last challenge en route to the summit. And at approximately 9:00 a.m. we stood atop the highest peak of the continent of Oceania.

However, summit number five was not yet completed. We still had to make it back down. While rappelling in snow and rain, I smacked my right elbow against a sharp rock wall. I knew that I had hit it hard, but because of the limited feeling in my arm due to my BPI, I was not aware that I had opened a huge gash in my elbow. I was also unaware that blood was running down my arm, filling my glove. When I removed my glove I was shocked to discover the deep red color saturating the lining. That sensitivity reduction, due to the nerve damage at birth, would again come into play on Everest.

Upon returning to Base Camp and bandaging the wound to my elbow, I paused to think. My wound could have been much worse, and I could have lost more blood. However, despite the lack of sensation in my arm, and the hardships that sometimes came with it, I felt privileged to be among the three out of every 1,000 babies born with a BPI. I was also thankful I had a mother who helped me realize that anything is possible, regardless of our challenges. Without this mindset and inherent predisposition toward creativity and problem solving that my birth injury fostered, I may not have been able to successfully tackle this mountain.

> *"Creativity is inventing, experimenting, growing, taking risks, breaking rules, making mistakes, and having fun."*
> —*Mary Lou Cook*

On the topic of problem solving, once settled in at Base Camp, I needed to make a few satellite phone calls to clients. One of those clients was the owner of a software company whose business I was in the process of selling. We had terms and conditions proposed by a buyer, and there was a large disparity between the offer and what my client was willing to accept. This "gap" seemed almost as large as the one I just crossed using the Tyrolean Traverse. It was my job to figure out a way to bridge the gap, and in the end with some creativity, we did.

Denise and I looked back at the summit of Carstensz Pyramid and began the long trek back through the jungle. I smiled even as my boots stuck in the thick mud and it began raining again. "I really did just figure out a way to climb the most technically challenging of the Seven Summits," I thought to myself. It was a major breakthrough, and there were no more apparent roadblocks preventing me from taking on the last two.

## *Step to the Summit*
# DISCOVER YOUR CREATIVITY

The lessons I learned growing up, about persistence and creatively overcoming obstacles, are precisely what has helped me to become successful in business during the past twenty years. After selling the family business and earning an MBA taking night classes, I began a new and exciting career in Mergers & Acquisitions in 1997. Helping other business owners sell their companies is extremely demanding, complex, and incredibly rewarding work; work that I still enjoy today as an investment banker and work that I performed full time (thanks to satellite communications technology) throughout my years climbing the Seven Summits.

One of the critical success factors in the M&A business is the ability to think creatively outside the box in order to identify a strategic fit with an appropriate acquiring company. Next, the right set of skills and tenacity is required to sell the target company and negotiate a myriad of detailed terms and conditions. Obstacles always arise during the sale process and a creative dealmaker can navigate a business owner through this journey just as an experienced mountain guide can find an alternate route around or out of a dangerous crevasse.

Again, the operative word is creativity. Use as many different keys and different combinations as required to unlock your creativity in finding a solution. If that doesn't work, look for an entirely different entrance or approach to the problem. Flexibility of mind and creativity are the keys that will unlock the door. The solution is there, but you must be persistent and perceptive enough to recognize it when it presents itself to you. I wasn't sure how I was going to tackle Carstensz

Pyramid, but Aron Ralston's prosthetic arm was the combination to that lock. It led me to find that hook in the hardware store aisle, and to create "The Claw." And then it guided me to the top of my fifth summit.

# BE DETERMINED & DISCIPLINED

*Choose an attitude of relentless resolve to achieve your objective.*
*Then be willing to endure some suffering to get there.*

---

*A*s I leaned into the final turn and peddled into the transition area, my pulse kicked up a notch. I was two-thirds of the way to finishing my first triathlon. I had completed the ocean swim, albeit slower than most of the others pulling with two strong arms, and plowed through the bike portion of the race. I had mentally rehearsed the final leg of the event and the process of quickly transitioning from cycling gear to running gear. With my shoes changed I sprang through the gates onto the run course with a confident stride. I could hear people yelling and saw them pointing at me as I ran past. My right arm is noticeably smaller and doesn't move like my left arm when I run, but rarely do people point. A bit rude of them, I thought to myself. I focused on setting my pace, concentrating on getting into my zone. It wasn't until I had passed scores of spectators that I realized the reason why they were yelling and pointing at me—I had forgotten to remove my bike helmet back in the transition area. Embarrassed and amused by my rookie move, I yanked it off my head, threw it in the bushes and kept running…

## TRAINING DAZE

Lots of people have asked me, "How exactly do you train to climb Mt. Everest?" In many ways, training for and then completing each of the Seven Summits thus far was building a foundation of mountaineering skills as well as physical stamina. You also need to be aerobically strong to handle the thin air environment of extreme high altitude mountaineering. So living at sea level, I decided the best way to get into prime condition was through endurance sports. I centered my training regimen on triathlons.

Preparing for a triathlon requires not only discipline, but also the determination to stay on top of a training schedule. In the best of scenarios, that training would be one's sole responsibility. But in the real world, we all have full lives—families, homes, and careers to maintain. As I began training for these races, I quickly discovered that I would need to achieve fine balances in order to keep not only my body in top notch physical shape, but my brain finely tuned as well.

> "We must all suffer from one of two pains: the pain of discipline or the pain of regret. The difference is discipline weighs ounces while regret weighs tons."
>
> —Jim Rohn

With each triathlon, I gained more knowledge and experience to help ready me for the next one. I was admittedly slow in my first race back in 2001; I was a newbie, riding a mountain bike instead of a road bike, and forgetting to remove my helmet. But I learned for the next one, and never made that mistake again. And then I learned something else for the one after that... and the one after that. Just as Mt. Kilimanjaro eventually led me to Mt. Everest, my first triathlon eventually led me to the greatest endurance race of all—The Ironman.

An Ironman Triathlon is a long-distance triathlon consisting of a 2.4-mile swim, a 112-mile bike ride and a full 26.2-mile marathon, raced in that order and without a break. Most Ironman events have a strict time limit of 17 hours to complete the entire race. It begins at 7 a.m. and all finishers must complete their marathon (the last leg) by midnight. The Ironman came to be from a debate as to whether runners were more fit than swimmers. In Hawaii in 1978, 15 men set out on an early February morning and only 12 finished the race. They named the winner "The Ironman," marking the beginning of the most coveted endurance test for any athlete.

I participated in 16 triathlons of shorter distances prior to competing in the Canada Ironman. As with each mountain, I methodically prepared myself for the task at hand. Training was key, and over the next six months I would swim a total of 135,000 yards, bike 2,500 miles and run 350 miles. I worked hard to maintain deadlines and keep ahead of client needs, as well as to be disciplined in following my training schedule. I remember after one particularly long and grueling early morning workout, I arrived at my office, sat down and began responding to some important emails. My body was spent; I had reached the point of utter exhaustion. My eyelids became heavy. Hoping my co-workers wouldn't notice, I quietly lay down on the floor behind my desk and just slept. I've never been accused of lying down on the job, but the moment that drool formed at the corner of my mouth, I must admit I was guilty. I woke up fatigued many days during these months, but managed to get out of bed and train at least six days and on average 15-20 hours per week. I completed the Canada Ironman in 12 hours and 36 minutes.

One day, while on a training ride with Denise, we were discussing our final two summits (Vinson and Everest), and I had an epiphany. I asked Denise; "Do you realize we have been given an opportunity to make an impact and accomplish something larger than ourselves and larger than Everest itself?" Before climbing Carstensz Pyramid, I had created a video, "Defining Life by Defying the Odds", to raise money for a charity close to my heart—the Challenged Athletes Foundation (CAF). Established in 1997, CAF is an organization that provides grants for prosthetic limbs and specialized sports equipment for children, American soldiers wounded in Iraq and Afghanistan, and other individuals with disabilities or missing limbs. But it's so much more than that. Like my mom did for me at an early age, CAF believes that involvement in sports at any level increases self-esteem, encourages independence and enhances quality of life.

It was thanks to CAF, and one of their athletes in particular whom I met in 1998, that I decided to attempt that very first triathlon. The athlete is Willie Stewart, or "One-Arm Willie" as he is affectionately known. Willie lost his left arm, just below the shoulder, in a construction accident. However it didn't stop him from swimming, biking, and running in triathlons, routinely decimating the vast majority of his able-bodied competitors in the sport. That was all the motivation I needed to realize the BPI impairing my right arm was just that, an impairment. After seeing all that Willie could accomplish with just one arm, I realized I had no excuses; at least I still had that other arm.

The epiphany on that training ride with Denise, was the realization we had a chance to create a mountain of awareness and charitable donations for CAF during our attempt to reach the highest point on Earth. The "Everybody to Everest Challenge" was born at that moment. We decided we would invite friends to join us in our journey to the Himalayas by hiking part way up the mountain while raising money for CAF. Our promotional flier designed to solicit interest from our personal contacts read in part:

*Here's your once in a lifetime chance to travel to Nepal, hike amongst stunning Himalayan peaks, stay in quaint Sherpa teahouses along the way, and get the behind the scenes experience of participating in a real Mt. Everest Expedition!*

- *You will have the opportunity to trek to the legendary Mt. Everest Base Camp at 17,500 feet.*

- *You will have the gratitude of your friends Paul & Denise who will be thrilled to see you as they spend 2 months in Nepal attempting to climb to the 29,029 foot summit of the earth's highest peak.*

- *You will be raising money for the Challenged Athletes Foundation and helping those less fortunate who may be physically unable to hike freely and explore the world.*

All of them would be required to pay their own costs of the trip, just as we were paying all of our own costs for the climbing expedition. We made it clear that without exception 100% of all fundraising dollars would go to CAF to help those in need. We hit the send button on a broadcast e-mail of the Everybody to Everest flier, and like an avalanche of altruism and positivity, the responses started pouring in. "Sounds like a great idea!" "I've always wanted to do something like this!" "Count me in!"

That summer, we held a kickoff party for sixty people at our home. We asked everybody what their biggest physical challenge had been up to that point in their lives and hands quickly shot in the air; "I've done a marathon!" "I've done a triathlon!" "I had a baby!" The excitement for the Everybody to Everest Challenge was palpable, and from there the initial roots of camaraderie among the group began to grow.

Perhaps the most inspiring moment was when Scout Bassett walked to the front of the room to talk as a representative for CAF and gave a heart wrenching account of how she lost her leg as a child. For the first seven years of her life, she was in a government orphanage in Nanjing, China, where she spent all of her time indoors mopping floors, washing dishes and caring for the younger children. She doesn't remember ever going outside and had no hopes for a better future.

She said she was abandoned at the orphanage in 1989 as a 1-year-old, badly burned from what appeared to be a chemical fire that scarred her skin and claimed her right leg up to mid-thigh. The adults at the orphanage made her a prosthetic leg out of leather belts and masking tape. Scout recalled it as the worst seven years of her life. She calls her adoption by an American family her miracle, and her involvement with CAF her second miracle. Thanks to generous donors to CAF, not only did she receive a new prosthetic leg but at the same time she also gained a new life. She now competes in a dozen triathlons and running races each year.

There was no stopping the momentum now. We began organizing training hikes, setting up fundraising campaigns and events and brought sponsors on board to donate gear. So many amazing things happened during this time, there is no other way to describe them other than divine intervention. On our second group training hike to a local peak in California called Mt. Baldy, we invited CAF athlete John Siciliano to join us. In 1993 John was struck by a drunk driver and lost his right leg above the knee. With the help of a specialized prosthetic leg, he went on to break track records and earn a spot on the U.S. Paralympic Team. He inspired millions at the 1996 Atlanta Games when his leg fell off during the gold medal race and he bravely picked himself up off the ground and hopped to the finish line on one leg. He didn't win a medal, but he managed to win the hearts and minds of all those who witnessed his sheer determination.

One thing John had never done before was hike to more than 10,000 feet on his prosthetic leg, as we had asked him to do. He made it to the top and we asked another hiker on the summit to take a photo for us of John and our entire group.

*Everybody to Everest training hike, Mt. Baldy, CA*

One of our Everybody to Everest group members was carrying a plastic Sport Chalet bag that he had set down when we took that group photo. Sport Chalet is a local sporting goods store that was one of the first outdoor products retailers to offer a wide array of equipment for the then-esoteric sports of rock climbing and backpacking—at the time (1960s) only available in catalogues. They are now a publicly traded company and have 55 stores in California, Nevada, Arizona and Utah. Craig, the kind individual who snapped our summit photo, recognized the bag and told us he worked for Sport Chalet and wanted to help our cause. He handed me his business card and it read Craig Levra, Chairman & Chief Executive Officer. And to think, if we hadn't asked him to take our photo, our support from Sport Chalet might never have happened.

At the end of the Everybody to Everest kickoff party, long before any of these hikes and activities began, our friend Jeff Roberts remarked, "I wonder who of this group is determined enough to sign on for all this training and fundraising and how many here will actually show up to Base Camp?" Well he did, along with twenty-two others.

> *"We must remember that one determined person can make a significant difference, and that a small group of determined people can change the course of history."*
> —*Sonia Johnson*

## *Step to the Summit*
# BE DETERMINED AND DISCIPLINED

Just as Aron Ralston provided me with the creative spark to design The Claw, and just as the inspiration to form the Everybody to Everest group flashed into my mind in a millisecond; the work and "perspiration" always encompasses the lion's share of the effort. Whether it's training for the Ironman or Mt. Everest, or whether it's building a thriving career or business, there are two principles required for success: determination and discipline. Creating a mindset of relentless resolve to achieve your objective is the first step. It's not enough to simply want to reach your goal, you must possess the grit and dogged determination to decide you will endure the necessary discomfort to actually get there. Once you fully convince and instruct your brain that the goal will in fact be pursued and achieved, the second step, discipline, becomes easier. If you are sufficiently determined, you won't need to draw as much from your willpower reserves to make the necessary sacrifices along the way.

> *"Genius is one percent inspiration and ninety-nine percent perspiration."*
> *—Thomas Edison*

Nonetheless, discipline is a skill that can and must be continually honed through practice. During the course of my Ironman/Everest training there were countless times when I felt that sitting on the couch and eating a bowl of ice cream would be far more enjoyable than lacing up my shoes and going for a 15-mile run. The concept of instant vs. delayed gratification can be used to continually create small incentives and rewards by telling yourself you can enjoy that ice cream and couch time after the workout. Another trick is to view every decision point in terms of whether or not it will move you up towards your goal. And if the chosen course of action doesn't move you up and closer towards your goal, it is moving you further down and away from your goal.

In addition to training and diet goals, these simple ideas work for all sorts of otherwise unpleasant but necessary tasks in business and in life, to which any successful and disciplined individual can attest. In fact, in Thomas J. Stanley's book "The Millionaire Mind," 733 millionaires were surveyed and asked to rate 30 success factors. It is no surprise that the #1 ranked response attributed to the success and wealth of these individuals was "being well disciplined." Not far behind on the list at #5 was "working harder than most people." I know I worked harder than most people while training for Everest, between managing my professional responsibilities, and simultaneously managing the Everybody to Everest Challenge, which was in many ways similar to running another business with 23 employees (in my spare time). Thankfully I had an excellent partner in Denise, who was instrumental in helping to manage the effort. Take the advice of Step #4 to heart, and you will find that the reward for hard work, determination, and discipline is the ability to enjoy a level of fulfillment and satisfaction that many never have the privilege to experience.

---------- *Step 5* ----------

# LEAD AND THEY WILL FOLLOW

*Leadership is a duty and a privilege bestowed upon all of us
from time to time. It is also a mindset that we are well-served
to maintain, regardless of our current role.*

---

## THE FROZEN CONTINENT

*"MEN WANTED...*
*For Hazardous Journey. Small wages, bitter cold,*
*long months of complete darkness, constant danger.*
*Safe return doubtful. Honour and recognition in case of success..."*
—Ernest Shackleton's 1914 Antarctic Expedition Recruiting Ad

With the Everybody to Everest machine roaring along on its own, in December of 2009, we packed our bags and headed to Punta Arenas at the southern tip of Chile, the jumping off point for Antarctica and our Vinson climb. The Vinson Massif is the highest peak of Antarctica, standing at 16,067 feet. It is located in the Ellsworth Mountain Range near the Ronne Ice Shelf, 750 miles from the South Pole. The average summertime temperature on Vinson is -20°F, not including the wind chill factor. While not our highest elevation to date, this remote location takes some serious organization and logistics to reach.

We first arrived in Punta Arenas with all of our gear and situated ourselves in a hotel overlooking the Straights of Magellan. Much like cramming for an important test, our first day consisted of a briefing by the owners of Antarctic Logistics & Expeditions, who explained the hazards of our impending journey. They also mentally prepared us for the extreme conditions where we were headed and the necessary safety precautions we needed to take. We were shown gruesome photos of several victims of frostbite, which was akin to watching the old "Red Asphalt" movie in driver's ed. class. We also had an opportunity to meet the others who would be making this epic odyssey to this frozen continent, including our guide Scott Woolums.

In business, every deal starts with a handshake. Shaking Scott Woolums' hand represented a different kind of a pact, for this one had a price tag of life on it. Since my BPI happens to affect my right arm, an initial handshake with me is often a surprising one. Any first impressions that are made, usually stem from a handshake, so when I clasped Scott's hand without the usual grip of a man my size, I'm sure he was making some assumptions.

In my profession, I'm constantly assessing skills, strengths and weaknesses, and character. In addition I'm always reading body language for clues. And now I was shaking the hand of the man with whom I would be entrusting not only my life, but the life of the woman I love. In addition to entrusting our lives to Scott on Vinson, we had recently decided that he would also lead our team on Everest. Scott's impressive and lengthy mountaineering resume included four successful Everest summits from both the North and South side routes. It occurred to me, while shaking hands with him at this initial meeting, that perhaps he was wondering if he had agreed to guide someone who may not have what it takes to make the journey? I would prove his suspicions wrong.

Getting to Vinson Base Camp is largely an exercise in patience, but also an experiment in luck. Our first step was to fly out from Punta Arenas, over the Straights of Magellan and the Drake Passage, to the interior of Antarctica. It is the most difficult and dangerous place in the world to fly, so one must wait for a near perfect weather forecast before attempting the four and a half hour journey. Just one year prior, our Polish climbing partner and friend Ania was held back two weeks and spent Christmas in Punta Arenas waiting day after day for a chance to fly. As luck would have it, weather was on our side and we prepared to take off for "the ice."

After gear and fuel drums were loaded through the rear belly ramp of the Ilyushin-76 Soviet era cargo jet, we boarded and prepared for a most unusual and memorable flight. In addition to the anxious, adrenaline-filled climbers on board, we shared space in the cargo hull with a team of 18 Argentine scientists who would be spending the next 14 months living at a research station studying this fascinating continent. Before takeoff, a member of the Russian flight crew made his very best attempt at an English language version of an emergency safety briefing. Despite his good intentions it was both frightening and comical at the same time. Perhaps it was due to the age of the aircraft or the labyrinth of exposed wires and cables overhead, or perhaps the warning signs all written in Cyrillic, with the exception of one panel with the English words printed "Emergency Rope." I tried comforting myself by thinking, "Well, we can't read any other safety warnings on board this Cold War flying relic, but at least we have an Emergency Rope!"

*Ilyushin-76 on the ice runway in Antarctica*

It was truly an astounding sight to see the immense ice sheets and icebergs scattered around the periphery of this continent and then to pass over the Antarctic Circle and head to a place where the sun never sets at this time of year during the Austral summer. We felt the plane descending and prepared ourselves for the dramatic touch down on the blue ice runway of the Patriot Hills Camp, which is the central base of operations for Antarctic Logistics & Expeditions. Keep in mind; we were on a plane that would be landing on a two-mile stretch of sheer ice without using any brakes. The plane would simply stop when it stopped. We cautiously stepped off the plane, taking care not to slip on the veritable ice rink below. The last thing we needed was to injure ourselves by falling before we even set foot on the mountain.

The next step was a flight on a much smaller twin engine turbo-prop aircraft fitted with skis for landing on the snow. This plane was designed and manufactured by the de Havilland Aircraft Company, and is known as the DHC–6 "Twin Otter." I felt a special connection to this rugged aircraft, as my Uncle Ian has been an aeronautical engineer for the company for over 25 years. Although we had the opportunity to fly in this same type of plane when we climbed Denali in 2007, it was just as much of a thrill to hear the powerful roar of its engines and once again be whisked up off the snow to another wintery alpine adventure.

It had been only four days since we had left the palm trees and sandy beach at our warm and sunny California home, and now to think we would be spending the days ahead in this frozen land living in a tent. The first few days at Base Camp are always a time to acclimatize. The altitude was 6,900 feet, but felt more like 10,000 due to the fact that the earth's atmosphere is thinner at the poles.

This was also a good time to get to know Scott a little better on a personal level. Just as he was assessing us, we were also assessing him. And what better way to get to know someone than to play Monopoly with him? Due to my profession, I'm a natural negotiator. In my Monopoly strategy, art definitely imitates life in the way I play. I'm a dealmaker; I like to trade property and make rent deals, loan cash to develop hotels, etc. Scott on the other hand, plays by the book; very strict and serious, and never wavering. It occurred to me that this was a trait to appreciate in the person who was organizing logistics and leading us on the most intense and dangerous expeditions of our lifetime.

One of our greatest experiences in Antarctica was an opportunity to ski on slopes where relatively few people in the world have ever skied. In an effort to acclimatize (and have a little fun), Denise and I hiked up the mountain from Base Camp and spent the afternoon carving tracks on some untouched powder in the blissful solitude of this remote place. It was strangely reminiscent of our helicopter skiing trip almost 14 years prior when Denise accepted my engagement ring and agreed to follow me wherever the turns in life may lead. Neither of us would have imagined we might find ourselves together in this magical winter wonderland at the bottom of the globe.

After two nights acclimatizing at Vinson Base Camp, our next step was to move up to Camp 1 at 9,000 feet. We hiked along the Branscomb Glacier carrying our tents, gear, food and fuel, some of which we hauled behind us in sleds to lighten the load on our backs. We also traveled roped together as a precaution for crevasses, and after my experience on Denali there was no need for Scott to convince me of the merits of this preventative measure. After a day of rest and acclimatization at Camp 1, we now focused on the task ahead of getting up to High Camp. Between us and that next targeted goal was a very steep 45° continuous climb with a 3,350 foot elevation gain. The route had already been set with fixed lines onto which we attached our ascenders to minimize the negative effect of a slip or fall here. Scott explained that this section of the climb is very similar to what we would encounter on Everest climbing the notoriously dangerous Lhotse Face, only a matter of months away.

We anticipated it would take 7-8 hours to reach the Vinson High Camp but the three of us moved quickly together as a team and made it to our destination in a brisk 4 hours and 45 minutes. All of the determination and

> *"Coming together is a beginning. Keeping together is progress. Working together is success."*
> *—Henry Ford*

discipline to maintain our rigorous training regimen was beginning to pay off, and we felt great. Arriving at High Camp in good health and form on any big mountain is a significant milestone, as the summit is usually well within reach—subject to the weather cooperating, of course. Our plan was to rest and acclimatize here at approximately 12,350 feet for a full day and make our summit attempt on December 23rd. Unfortunately that plan was abruptly altered upon Scott receiving word from Base Camp that a storm system would soon be moving in to our area.

The three of us crammed together in a tent for the night and prepared to leave for the summit in the morning, hoping to beat the storm. When we awoke, we unzipped the tent door to near whiteout conditions and a light snow was already beginning to fall. The Antarctic storm had arrived early. Scott made the executive decision as our leader that we would go ahead anyway.

As we made our way towards the summit in the increasingly cold, windy, and snowy weather, the Challenged Athletes Foundation was not far from our minds. Earlier we had received notification by satellite phone that our single largest donation of $5,000 came in to CAF. Its significance was huge as we realized at that moment what we were doing was having a tremendous impact. Just as we were struggling through precarious climbing conditions these were also precarious economic times. This made each fundraising success all the more impressive and gratifying. We were feeling awkward knowing friends had lost their jobs and we were asking them to donate, but we reminded ourselves that we live in a country of great abundance and people are willing to make small sacrifices and withstand temporary hardships in order to help those in greater need. We were living proof that if you have a worthy goal and believe in it with all of your might, you'll get through the storm. And at that moment, we needed to get ourselves through the Antarctic storm and get our banner bearing the CAF logo to the summit of the Vinson Massif.

We did make it to the summit and safely back down all the way to Vinson Base Camp by Christmas Eve. Cloud cover prevented flying out so we thoroughly appreciated our leisure time to enjoy a well earned meal and a toast to our success with a coveted stockpile of Chilean boxed wine. We made a few satellite phone calls to wish a Merry Christmas to family back home, and also took the opportunity to reflect upon our next step. We had just carried the CAF banner to the highest point on the continent of Antarctica, and now we needed to get it to the top of the world!

• • • • •

────── *Step to the Summit* ──────
# LEAD AND THEY WILL FOLLOW

During our Christmas Eve celebrations in the frozen tundra of Antarctica, we had ample time to talk with members of two other small climbing teams who were on the mountain with us. One was a group of four Japanese climbers including a man named Ochiai Masaji, who had lost all ten of his fingers to frostbite on Everest earlier that year. Clearly he must have recognized the risk as his fingers became cold, we thought to ourselves. Why didn't he or his team leader say or do something that could have prevented this massively debilitating injury that will severely impact his functioning in life forever? Ochiai previously had full use of all ten fingers, I am grateful for five, and now he has none. The site of those nubs on his hands was permanently seared into my memory. This later led to a very serious private discussion between Denise and me about whether one of us would continue onward while climbing Everest if the other couldn't make it or had to turn around. If I reached the summit and Denise didn't, or vice versa, would it be an empty success? And more importantly, what if one of us needed the help of the other and we weren't there? We're a team, and I kept reminding myself that no summit is worth the sacrifice Ochiai made losing all of his fingers.

We were confident in our partnership and our commitment together as a husband/wife team, but we also realized there would be others involved and important decisions affecting our lives would be made by our leader Scott. We had no reason to doubt him; on the contrary, our experience in Antarctica served to build our confidence and trust in his experience, skills, and decision-making abilities. Hopefully he gained a similar trust in our abilities and future contributions as members of our Everest team.

> *"The task of the leader is to get his people from where they are to where they have not been."*
> *—Henry Kissinger*

These are important considerations that apply not only to a climbing team, but are equally applicable to business and life as well. We are all members or leaders of various teams throughout life (company, family, community, etc.) and in order to have a winning team there must be a shared leadership responsibility among all of the members. Leadership is more than just a position or title of one individual; it's an overriding attitude and state of mind. Looking closely at the most effective leaders throughout history, one will find a broad variety of leadership styles and personality types which work well in their own ways. Delving deeper however, chances are good that certain common traits exist and are shared by all. Some of those attributes include: integrity of character, competence through specific skills and strengths, and a high degree of energy and enthusiasm. Other traits shared by the very best leaders are those already covered in the previous Steps to the Summit: dreaming big and stepping up, living courageously, discovering your creativity, and exercising determination and discipline. The remaining Steps to the Summit also represent proven qualities of effective leaders. Focus on expanding these important components of your character and not only will you become a better leader, you will soon find yourself standing on the Summit!

# BE PREPARED

*Before undertaking a significant event, prepare for and accept in your mind
the consequences of the worst possible outcome. Upon doing so you will
move forward with the confidence and grace of a champion.*

## PACK YOUR BAGS

The peak of all peaks now lay directly in our line of sight. Six summits reached, one remaining. We had just dusted off the frost from our trip to Antarctica, and now had three short months to prepare for our trip to Everest. So, how exactly does one prepare for a journey to the top of the world?

Professionally, I had some heavy duty preparations to make before leaving. I had primed my clients and my firm well in advance for my two-month long absence, and tied up as many loose ends as possible. However, the largest deal of my career was still hanging in the balance. I was representing the owners of a medical device company and had negotiated a $115 million transaction for the founder to sell the business. It would mean a practically inconceivable amount of wealth for this industrious immigrant entrepreneur, and a commission for me that would more than pay for our Everest expedition. I had been working on this deal for over a year, and day after day put most of my time and energy into making it happen before we left. I was concerned; the buyer should have been moving faster and the deal should have been closed by now. And then the fateful call came from the buyer; they were no longer comfortable with the acquisition under the terms of the letter of intent. The deal was off.

I learned many years ago in this business to be prepared for unexpected curve balls of this nature. This didn't change the fact that I was, of course, still devastated by the news. But at least I had maintained good relationships with the four competing buyers who had all made offers on the company earlier, and I was able to salvage the situation and rekindle interest from one of them. The work was about to begin all over again, and I was supposed to leave for Everest in less than a month! Fortunately I had also prepared for a circumstance like this by enlisting a colleague to participate alongside me on the deal from day one. He was up to speed on the nuances of the negotiations and my client was comfortable with him. It was time for me to hand over the reins and trust my colleague to make the right decisions on my behalf, and hopefully get the deal back on track. Being unable to close this large transaction as anticipated was a big blow on many levels, but after squaring this away I felt I was prepared for anything and everything that could possibly come next.

Denise and I also had to be extra prepared for the 23 other people who would be joining us on part of our journey—the Everybody to Everest group we had assembled. These amazing people were putting all of their faith in us, they had raised an enormous amount of money for our cause, and they would be taking three weeks off from work. Most importantly, they would be leaving their family and friends to go on a somewhat precarious journey. We simply couldn't let them down.

Since we would be leaving three weeks ahead of the group to start acclimatizing to the high altitude, we needed the help of a seasoned professional guide to lead their 10-day trek up to Base Camp. A woman named Heidi Kloos from Ridgway, Colorado came highly recommended. Heidi had 15 years of experience guiding big mountains around the world, had led ten expeditions up Denali, a similar number of trips up Aconcagua, and had climbed extensively in Nepal. She was also involved with a program that helped disabled athletes learn to ski and climb. Much like CAF, the Telluride Adaptive Sports Program enriches the lives of people with disabilities by providing therapeutic recreational opportunities that would otherwise be beyond their reach. Learning of Heidi's dedication to helping challenged athletes realize their dreams and achieve their goals, I knew she would be the perfect person to lead our Everybody to Everest group.

As our own departure neared, we continued our preparation with intensive training hikes, final travel plans, and spent each evening lining up our gear in our spare bedroom. We worked our way through a seven-page packing checklist, organizing to ensure we would have the vital equipment needed to get safely to the summit and back. We sharp-

> *"Before anything else, preparation is the key to success."*
> *—Alexander Graham Bell*

ened our crampons and ice axes, gathered lithium batteries for head-lamps (they last longer in the extreme cold), and lined up trekking shoes, insulated expedition boots, and an array of warm hats, jackets, and sleeping bags. As I stacked gloves and summit mittens, I had visions of Ochaiai's ten stubs where his fingers used to be.

My determination to be fully prepared so as not to have anything like that happen to me or Denise, or anyone on our team, was in the forefront of my mind as we set out pile after pile of clothing and equipment. The best and warmest pair of summit gloves available on the market were $159; that's $15.90 a finger, we rationalized. Worth every penny! When all was said and done, between the two of us, this expansive heap of gear would fill four oversized duffel bags and weigh nearly 200 pounds.

*All geared up! Packing for Mt. Everest*

Along with the seven-page checklist came several legal forms to fill out. One form in particular was a blunt reminder of the dangerous journey upon which we were about to embark. It was titled, "Body Disposal & Repatriation Form."

- *If you die on the mountain above 7,800 meters (25,800 feet) your body will be left at that location.*

- *If you die on the mountain above 5,300 meters (17,500 feet) your body may be put in a crevasse and POSSIBLY marked with a rock cairn in a respectful manner by your expedition team members.*

- *If you die lower on the mountain it might be possible to get your body down where it could be cremated by the locals. This will cost several thousand dollars including the cost of recovery labor, transport and body preparation, wood and appropriate donations to the local monastery. This cost is usually between $5,000 and*

*$10,000. It will not be possible to bring your ashes home because of the cremation process.*

- *If you die down lower on the mountain or on the trek to base camp, it might be possible to get your body down for repatriation to your home country. If you elect repatriation of your body it would be via helicopter and would be quite complicated and expensive, and might take several weeks.*

At the bottom of the page, we were required to indicate our preference for repatriation, cremation by the locals, or to leave our body on the mountain. A spouse's signature was necessary as well, so with a deep breath, Denise and I signed the forms for one another. I thought about one more important thing that I needed to prepare. It was something I knew I really needed to do, but had never taken the time to assemble up to this point in my life—a last will and testament.

The weeks leading up to our departure for Nepal were a blur. We did our final gear additions and began to say goodbye to all of our family and friends. It was truly a roller coaster ride of emotions. Then, less than one week before our departure, we received some troubling news. Heidi Kloos, the guide who was supposed to lead the trek of our Everybody to Everest group up to Base Camp, had been reported missing while on a hike near her home in Colorado. She had set out with her dog Menke to scout an area for some ice climbing and, when she didn't return as planned, a search and rescue team was sent to look for her. The fear was that she had been caught in an avalanche. But she wasn't in an area particularly prone to avalanches and was probably more mindful than most of taking safety precautions and assessing snow stability. An avalanche had killed her fiancé back in 1999.

Nonetheless a large accumulation of snow had built up far above where she was hiking, and its immense weight broke loose at an inopportune time. They found Menke anxiously whimpering next to Heidi's pack among a massive pile of avalanche debris. After countless hours of digging well into the night, the search and rescue team decided to go home for a break. However, Menke refused to leave. The next day, they finally discovered Heidi's body buried beneath five feet of snow.

We had spent weeks physically preparing for our journey but with Heidi's passing we realized that we also needed to emotionally prepare. We were headed to one of the most dangerous mountains in the world and one of our guides had just died in an avalanche right here at home. We had an extremely hard time breaking the news to our group that their guide had just been killed. They took it amazingly well and they were surprisingly reassuring. One of our members Karen Robinson wrote us a touching email, "…R.I.P. Heidi, you will be our guide from above." Still, it was a bitter pill to swallow; we hadn't yet set foot on the mountain and were already mourning the tragic loss of a vibrant young spirit.

Stunned by the loss of Heidi, we did our best to put smiles on our faces and headed out to a CAF fundraising event organized by my sister Tina, which also doubled as a Bon Voyage party. We donned our puffy Marmot down suits and performed a choreographed dance to the Black Eyed Peas song "Let's Get it Started!" It definitely lightened the mood for us and provided fun entertainment, but many of our friends and family in attendance couldn't help but wonder, "Could this possibly be the last time we will see them?" Let's hope not, it would be a shame to have our embarrassing dance routine be the last visual impression we left on them!

In the midst of this light-hearted and silly fun, losing Heidi showed us that there was always the possibility—the real possibility— that it might be the last time we would see our friends. We were about to embark on the riskiest adventure we have ever attempted. And it is indeed a fact that people die on Everest every year. You actually need to go back more than three decades to 1977 to find a year when nobody perished. One can prepare for most things in life, but can you ever truly prepare for that sobering reality?

We stopped at my mom's on Easter Sunday to share one last dinner with both of our families before heading to the airport. It was very emotional seeing our moms for the last time, and it was extremely difficult to see them crying as we hugged them goodbye. I had also unintentionally given my mother additional fuel for tears by leaving a special envelope with her. She knew what was inside. So, with that envelope containing our signed wills in her hand, we waved goodbye and with tear-filled eyes we drove off to the airport to catch our flight to Nepal.

• • • • •

*Step to the Summit*
## BE PREPARED

As the founder of the international Scouting movement in 1908, Lord Robert Baden-Powell declared that two simple words be the motto of the Boy Scouts: "Be prepared." Being prepared isn't just about having warm enough gloves for the summit. Through my involvement with the organization growing up, I learned that he wanted each Scout to be ready in mind and body for any struggles, and to meet with a strong heart whatever challenges might lie ahead. Be prepared for life —to live happily and without regret, knowing that you have done your best.

> *"The fear of death follows from the fear of life. A man who lives fully is prepared to die at any time."*
> *—Mark Twain*

Later in my business career I learned another lesson or trick to mentally prepare for a significant event. Whether it is a job interview, or an important presentation to a prospective client or board of directors, one must ask a single question. "What is the absolute worst outcome that could happen here?" In business, that "worst outcome" is that you don't get the job, the client or board says no, or you lose a specific sum of money. Once you accept the worst-case scenario and realize that it's not that bad, this simple act of mental preparation provides a tremendous amount of confidence in moving forward.

In most cases those scary things in life you are preparing for are not going to result in death. Perhaps the death of the single largest business deal of your lifetime might occur as I experienced, but you will live. Of course, in our upcoming challenge on Everest, death was in fact a real possibility. We were by no means accepting that outcome but, we had now mentally addressed this risk. I believe it is a valuable exercise for everybody to periodically stop and reflect upon how you have lived your life up to this point. If it were to unexpectedly end tomorrow, are you prepared? Would you have done certain things differently? Are you proud of the way you have conducted yourself in business, and in dealings with friends, family, and strangers along your path? Could you have done more? And do you need to apologize to anybody, ask them for forgiveness, or grant forgiveness to somebody who has hurt you?

Being prepared in this manner is a vitally imperative Step to the Summit. If you are truly desirous of achieving great successes in your business and in life, stop right now and take a moment to reflect upon and write down your responses to the above questions. Jot them down right on this page if you wish, it will be a liberating experience for you, and a necessary step in order to give you the power to go higher!

---

*Step 7*

# DON'T WORRY BE HAPPY

*Even during times of great hardships, always remember to take pause and show gratitude for what you have. Research shows you will accomplish more and enjoy greater success with a positive state of mind.*

---

## GOING TO KATHMANDU

We were here. We had left our home, our families, and our responsibilities and had made the journey to Nepal and the start of what we hoped would be an achievement of a lifetime. We were attempting our seventh summit—Mt. Everest, the crown of the world. Standing tall at 29,029 feet, this massive mountain was going to be our home for the next two months. Although they have improved in recent years, the statistics I had read previously were daunting and ran through my head like a ticker tape: "Thirty percent of climbers who attempt the summit of Mt. Everest succeed... Out of every ten who reach the summit, one will die trying... Some 200-plus people still lie dead among the slopes of the mountain..." I inhaled deeply and stepped off the plane.

Arrival in Kathmandu is usually a chaotic experience for most people, considering its third world population of 1.4 million people packed into less than twenty square miles, not to mention the cows and chickens competing for space on the narrow city roads. However, for us it seemed like a peaceful respite from the hectic pace we had been running before our departure. After all the months of physical and mental preparation, it was now time to clear our minds, relax and simply get up on the mountain and climb.

It also helped that this was our second trip to Kathmandu. Two years prior we were fortunate enough to have been invited to the wedding of a friend in Calcutta, India. We took advantage of the opportunity since we were so close in proximity, and extended the trip in order to scope out Everest in person on a ten-day trek. We even stayed at the same hotel in Kathmandu on both trips, the famous Yak & Yeti where legendary mountaineers Edmund Hillary, Tenzing Norgay, Rob Hall, Scott Fischer, Ed Visteurs, Reinhold Messner and others have all stayed. It was also where our Everybody to Everest team would be staying.

In most commercially guided expeditions, members are usually meeting each other for the first time immediately before the climb begins, many times in a hotel lobby. This was the case in 1996 when the members of the ill-fated expeditions of Rob Hall and Scott Fisher assembled. John Krakauer dramatically recounted the tales in his acclaimed book "Into Thin Air." Dysfunctional climbing teams were, in part, to blame for a catastrophic death toll that claimed a total of 15 lives on Everest that season. We decided to take a different approach and formed our own team. It was a team of individuals we knew and trusted and with whom we felt comfortable. Having this familiarity with one another was reassuring, particularly since we were setting out on a journey filled with so many other unknown factors.

The first member of our group was 37 year-old Ania Lichota, our Polish friend whom we met in Russia four years earlier and with whom we subsequently climbed three of the Seven Summits. She lives in London and works as a director in international banking. Denise and I had spent many stormy days and nights crammed into a tent with Ania. You definitely get to know a lot about a person's values and character (among other personal habits) living in such close quarters. We also experienced numerous episodes of hysterical laughter together, sometimes as a result of her less than perfect understanding of the English language and some of our colloquialisms.

Next was 39 year-old Vivian Rigney, an Irishman with a great spirit. He lived in New York and was working as an executive coach. Ania had climbed with Vivian before so she knew he had the requisite strength and climbing skills. Because of his background and professional experience, he was always a welcomed companion for an intellectual business discussion on the trail or over a cup of tea. I enjoyed discussing clients with him, and he appreciated my need to make occasional business calls on the satellite phone from Base Camp.

The fifth member of our climbing team was a late addition by the name of Cindy Abbott, a 51 year-old mother and university professor living in Irvine, California. She had originally planned to climb with Russell Brice's company Himalayan Experience. After seeing him featured on the Discovery Channel series "Everest—Beyond the Limits," she was inspired to climb the "Big E" and sent in a deposit and completed the application process to climb with Russell's expedition. However as soon as Cindy found out we had formed an Everest team with Scott Woolums and the Colorado-based expedition company Mountain Trip, she arranged to make a switch and joined our team because she had previously done some training climbs with Scott. She had far less climbing experience than the rest of us, which was a bit troubling, but she was sufficiently determined.

And then of course our climbing guides: Scott Woolums, whom we had bonded with in Antarctica, and Bill Allen, co-owner of Mountain Trip, whom we had met years prior while climbing with his company on Denali. Bill has guided extensively in Nepal and around the world, including 22 Denali climbs, a dozen Aconcagua ascents, six Carstensz Pyramid trips, and several Vinson expeditions. All in all we had a pretty cohesive group, which was crucial considering we would be spending the next two months together. It was by design and there was less uncertainty involved as compared to simply joining a hodgepodge group of climbers on a larger expedition. We had done that before and sometimes those situations work out well and sometimes they don't. The wrong individuals on a team can add unnecessary drama and danger.

*Mt. Trip climbing team:*
*Scott Woolums, Bill Allen, Ania Lichota, Cindy Abbott, Vivian Rigney, and us*

Speaking of danger, now that our team and all of our bags of gear were together in Kathmandu, it was time for our flight to Tenzing/Hillary Airport in the village of Lukla at 9,350 feet. The airport is named for Sir Edmund Hillary and Tenzing Norgay Sherpa, the first persons to successfully summit Everest in 1953 (and who also made the construction of the airport possible). We later learned that this airstrip is ranked as #1 among the "Ten Most Extreme Airports" in the world on a recent History Channel special by the same name. The airport is characterized by frequent crosswinds, its short runway only 1,500 feet long, and the fact that it is carved into the mountainside at a 12% gradient (which makes for an interesting uphill landing). The vertical wall at the end of the runway makes an aborted landing impossible. As a pilot your options are to either land successfully on the first attempt—or crash. We ended up waiting seven hours for good enough weather in which to fly, and with the exception of a very bumpy ride and an even scarier landing, things were off to a relatively smooth start. Our journey to Base Camp had begun.

After organizing our gear and porters, some of our bags were sent straight to Base Camp on the backs of yaks, which are large, longhaired bovines found throughout the Himalayas and which are an important part of the Sherpa culture and commerce. We put our personal packs on our back and set out hiking along a familiar trail. It was definitely nice to start trekking, and a peaceful, happy feeling washed over me as we looked across the magical region and heard the faint ringing of yak bells off in the distance. They each seemed to chime their own melodies keeping in time with the animals' steps as the yaks trudged up the mountain. Vast terraced fields with quaint Sherpa homes nestled in the hillsides with views of the majestic Himalayan peaks towering above laid out before me like an artist's rendering. The clear Himalayan mountain air and the fresh scent of the pine forest let us know we were somewhere special.

> *"If you want to live a happy life, tie it to a goal, not to people or things."*
> *—Albert Einstein*

It was incredibly surreal to be able to experience the natural beauty and Sherpa culture twice in our lifetime; I felt quite privileged, considering very few Westerners even get one opportunity to visit this spiritual and remote area—let alone two opportunities. What made the afternoon even more special was being in this place again with Denise, thinking of the memories shared together here before, and then conceptualizing the magnitude of the undertaking we had returned here to tackle. After all the training and preparation, after all the thinking and talking about it, we were here. And we were happy.

We stopped for the first night at one of the many Sherpa teahouses that provide a comfortable resting place along the trail to Base Camp. Our happiness was briefly interrupted when the porters delivered our bags. Denise's bag was covered in a white powdery substance. We nervously opened it and found that the entire two-pound container of our electrolyte replacement energy drink powder had been crushed and spilled throughout her bag. She was understandably aggravated and we spent most of the evening cleaning out the contents of her bag and scooping up the powder to save what was left. I couldn't help but wonder if that frustrating event was a meaningful occurrence to remind me not to worry about things of small significance, but to focus on practicing my happiness.

We awoke the next morning and hiked up to Namche Bazaar at 11,300 feet in the Solu Khumbu Valley. It is known as the "Gateway to the Himalayas" and is the main trading center for the Khumbu region. We decided to hike above the village to 12,600 feet and were able to get our first sighting of the mighty mountain. We chatted with some of the local Sherpas and chuckled as they gossiped about a rumor that Brad Pitt was on the mountain. It was like we had a little piece of home. There are no cars or bikes nor many other modern conveniences here in these remote mountains, but yet they had an Internet café. So we checked in with home at the rate of 450 rupees/hour, or about $7.00. We later saw these prices escalate to 1,200 rupees/hour or about $20.00, at the more remote and higher villages along the trail. We also had our first shower of the trip here in Namche. We knew these would be in short supply for the next two months, so we definitely saw the value of this gift. Knowing that all of our other team members were on this journey without their spouses, I felt incredibly lucky to be sharing this experience with Denise (not to mention the shower)!

*Village of Namche Bazaar & view of Kwangde Peak*

Our next day's trek was to the Tengboche Monastery that sits atop a hill at 12,687 feet above the confluence of the Dudh Kosi and the Imja Khola rivers, with a clear view of Everest. As the story goes, about 350 years ago, a high priest of Khumbu named Lama Sangwa Dorje pronounced Tengboche to be a religious site and promised that it would one day be home to a monastery. In 1923, that is precisely what happened. Today Tengboche Monastery marks one of the most influential religious centers for Sherpa culture, with 35 monks calling it home. It was quite an experience for us to hear the low-pitched rhythmic melody of the chants and prayers of the monks in this candle-lit, incense-filled sanctuary where so many other climbers before us

> *"Thousands of candles can be lit from a single candle, and the life of the candle will not be shortened. Happiness never decreases by being shared."*
> —*Buddha*

67

have come to receive blessings. It was almost as if you could feel the history and spirit of great climbers like Mallory, Irvine, Hillary and Norgay and the hundreds who came after them. We received our blessings with ceremonial Kata scarves symbolizing good luck and safe passage up the slopes of Everest.

We also counted our blessings near Tengboche when a German woman affected by HAPE (High Altitude Pulmonary Edema) came stumbling through the doors of the teahouse lodge where we were staying. As luck would have it, a group of doctors happened to be staying at this lodge and quickly sprang into action to assess her current state. Using a small diagnostic gauge called a pulse oximeter, they determined her blood oxygen saturation level was an alarmingly low 57%. At sea level this reading should be close to 100%. They immediately gave her an injection of dexamethasone. Fortunately the doctors also happened to be carrying with them a Gamow Bag. They put her inside this portable hyperbaric chamber and pumped it full of pressurized air. It brought the effective altitude inside the bag down 5,000 feet to 7,500 feet. The doctors stayed up with her all night pumping air manually into the bag. By morning the woman's blood oxygen saturation level had improved to 86%. It was clear to all of us that without this critical and timely assistance, the German woman likely would have been dead. She was evacuated by helicopter in the morning.

It was onward and upward to Dingboche at 14,800 feet. We were elated to find our own "honeymoon suite" at the Snow Lion Lodge, another perk to being a climbing couple. And by "honeymoon suite" I mean a 10'x10' wooden structure reminiscent of a backyard tool shed. It was actually Mingma the proprietor's quarters, and she generously loaned it to us to offer some additional comfort and privacy over the other dormitory style rooms in the main lodge. We weren't expecting much privacy during this trip and looked at each other like giddy teenagers when we learned of our good fortune. We were definitely happy, albeit laboring to catch our breath at times as we were slowly adjusting to the increasingly higher altitude.

After a few days' rest at Dingboche, we were back on the trail moving up to Lobuche at 16,175 feet—getting closer and closer to Base Camp.

It is a long, laborious hike to Lobuche taking the better part of the day to complete. We shared the narrow, winding trail with yaks ferrying food and supplies. Along the way we passed through a very sacred place adorned with many Chortens, which are stone memorials to those who have died on the mountain. It is an incredible mix of emotions seeing more than 200 of these Chortens, including memorials for the well-known guides Rob Hall and Scott Fischer who died in the 1996 tragedy.

You walk with a sense of peace and happiness at what you are doing, but then sadness washes over you as you realize what these memorials truly signify. There is an eerie silence as climbers walk on this hallowed land. It also commands from them a tremendous respect for the mountain, reminding climbers of the dangers they will soon face above Base Camp. As we stepped through history, Scott made one somber comment, "None of these people thought they would die on Everest."

• • • • •

*Step to the Summit*
## DON'T WORRY BE HAPPY

From the tragic loss of Heidi Kloos before the trip to dancing in down suits to the Black Eyed Peas, to wrapping up business deals, the emotional farewell to family and the handoff of our wills, each moment leading up to this great adventure seemed in itself a monumental event. But being on the streets of Kathmandu, with poverty everywhere yet witnessing smiles on more faces than in any other third world country we had visited, is what brought everything into perspective. In life, the importance of accepting what you have and appreciating it *in the moment* is of greater value than any material success. Life and fortunes can change in an instant, whether from an avalanche, a plane crash, or walking across the street to work. Practice being happy and be thankful for the privilege of being alive and healthy.

> **"Happiness is not something ready made. It comes from your own actions."**
> **—Dalai Lama**

We can learn a lot from the Nepalese people and Sherpas about consciously practicing to keep oneself in a positive, happy state of mind, in spite of the chaos and uncertainty that seem to be swirling around. Similarly we can benefit from the knowledge of the Dalai Lama himself by accepting the fundamental premises from his book "The Art of Happiness." He says first and foremost "the purpose of life is happiness." He goes on to say that "happiness can be achieved through the systematic training of our hearts and minds, through reshaping our attitudes and outlook." An ironic by-product of applying this skill to life is the degree to which a relaxed, optimistic, accepting, and happy state of mind actually improves performance—and health.

A 53-page in-depth study by the American Psychological Association published by professors Lyubomirsky, King, and Diener entitled "The Benefits of Frequent Positive Affect," concluded that happiness actually CAUSES success, rather than simply the common belief of the opposite, that success is what causes happiness. Of course success MAY bring happiness as a result, but we all can cite examples of seemingly successful people who are not happy. Therefore it is far better to start out happy, and as the research demonstrates, you will then improve your chances of being successful …and attaining your next Step to the Summit.

# HAVE A LITTLE FAITH

*Sometimes you just need to let go and relinquish control. Faith is a potent*
*force that will carry you through the most difficult of challenges.*

## IS THERE A LAMA IN THE HOUSE?

As we took our first steps into Base Camp, we were in awe of the breath-taking sight that lay before our eyes. We were walking into a vast tent city canvassed by a backdrop of the most spectacular mountain scenery in the world. For Everest is not the only Himalayan giant to impress us on this trek. The great peaks of Nuptse, Lhotse, Lho La and Pumori surround this sprawling tent community. They tower above like colossal guardians simultaneously protecting and warning the tiny human inhabitants camping at their feet. Probably the most befitting description—we were mere mortals unworthy of standing in this heavenly sanctuary of the gods.

As we stepped along the broken glacial moraine through the other expedition sites, we bumped into a familiar face. We were shocked and pleasantly surprised to see Tim Rippel, who was our heli-skiing guide fourteen years ago when I proposed to Denise in the Canadian Rockies. Tim was at Base Camp guiding a climbing team for his own expedition company, Peak Freaks. It was great to reconnect with him after so many years and share another milestone adventure by climbing Everest at the same time. Seeing Tim's rugged but friendly smile and hearing his quirky Canadian accent surfaced a rush of vivid memories and emotions for me. I couldn't help being catapulted back to that moment all those years ago, when I got down on one knee on another faraway mountain and asked a question that would change my life forever. Back then I definitely could not have predicted that those first turns Denise and I took down the powdery slopes would eventually lead us here, to Mt. Everest.

After chatting with Tim, we made our way to the base of the majestic Khumbu Icefall, where Mountain Trip's camp had been set up. What an impressive sight to see. Our jaws dropped as we stepped inside the huge Mountain Hardware dome tent. It was a literal command center. Scott was busy setting up electronics, solar panels, batteries, lighting, a stereo with speakers, and communications equipment including satellite phones, a modem, laptop computers, and radios for our climbing team. Tables with neatly organized stacks of food and condiments lined the edge of the tent, and any necessity you could think of was there. It was staggering to think that all of this gear made its way from the States to the base of this remote Himalayan mountain that would be our new home for the next six weeks or so. It was also difficult to process that all of it had made its way up the mountain on the powerful back of a porter or a yak.

*Everest Base Camp & Mt. Trip dome tent – 17,500 feet*

It was surreal to think that the combined climbers, support teams and Sherpa staff creating this temporary community totaled upwards of 600 people. Based on the twenty-three permits issued this season (each permit allows a maximum of ten people), we estimated there would be about 200 climbers on the mountain. I couldn't help but wonder how many of us would overcome the odds and actually reach the summit. Unquestionably, everybody there had trained and prepared and planned to be successful, but statistically the majority would not make it to the top. And almost certainly, some would never make it home. I hoped and prayed that we would not end up one of those statistics.

On the surface, this harsh rocky terrain reminds me of photos we have seen of the moon, but underneath the scores of tents scattered about was actually the slow moving ice of the Khumbu Glacier. We were literally going to be living on a moving, frozen river. A moving, frozen river at 17,500 feet where there is only one-half the oxygen we were used to breathing. Aside from all the other incredible statistical information and voluminous research that has been done on Mt. Everest, this fact alone is quite an interesting one. This majestic place that is inhabited by hundreds of people for two months of the year, is in fact on unstable ground. Not only were we climbing unpredictable terrain, we were camping on it as well.

Before continuing to unpack and get settled in our own personal tent, we met Purba Surki Sherpa who played two very important roles on our team. The role we were most interested in at the moment was his duty as a Base Camp cook. Knowing we would be tired and hungry from our long hike up from Lobuche, Purba Surki already had a hot meal waiting for us—garlic, ginger and mushroom soup and cheese sandwiches with fries. It was quickly becoming obvious that a seemingly inhospitable place was made surprisingly comfortable with modern conveniences and a Sherpa crew of 20, whom we would quickly grow to love like a family.

The Sherpa culture is fascinating to me, and honestly, theirs is a society from which we can learn what is really important in life. While most of us spend our days chasing what we perceive to be important, they appreciate the simple pleasures, and seem intimately connected to a higher power. It's easy to see this because it is written all over their faces. They have witnessed so much death and hardship living in these villages in their stone houses and with so little of the modern conveniences we're accustomed to, yet they are at peace, and it is readily apparent. In Asian cultures, there is a spiritual belief that the act of physically moving higher will bring you closer to your ancestors and to God. One can't get much higher than where we stood then, and where we were headed. The Sherpas are, simply put, happy to be here.

> *"One life is all we have and we live it as we believe in living it. But to sacrifice what you are and to live without belief, that is a fate more terrible than dying."*
> —*Joan of Arc*

The Sherpa culture emerged in the mid-sixteenth century from the Khams region of Tibet. They were farmers, making their livings in the fields—harvesting crops and raising livestock such as yaks and cows. In the nineteenth century, the Sherpas began using their convenient location between Tibet and Nepal to trade their wares, with the yak as their main transport animal. When the Irish potato became a popular crop across the world, the Sherpa people adopted it as their main staple crop and it greatly enriched their region. The Khumbu villages were established, and today the potato continues to bring them revenue (not to mention it being our main staple on Everest). In later years, mountaineering and tourism would become extremely lucrative industries, largely credited to the 1953 conquest of Mt. Everest by Tenzing Norgay Sherpa and Sir Edmund Hillary, and it is in fact their main economy today. As I shook hands with my new neighbors, it was easy to see they are a people steeped in history, and incredibly proud of their lineage.

The Sherpas had already set up tents for our team and Denise and I picked the very last one in the row of seven for privacy. It had a magnificent view of the Khumbu Icefall and Nuptse Peak from the front door. As we crawled in, it hit me that this was primarily where we would be living for the next six weeks. We looked at each other excitedly, eager to continue on our journey and also apprehensive at the enormity of it all. We unpacked and organized some of our gear and settled in for our first night of sleep. The magnitude of our planned endeavor was ever present, and I lay awake for a while thinking of what was to come in the weeks ahead, listening to Denise's rhythmical breathing as she slept next to me. I silently said a small prayer for our safety and drifted off to sleep.

Avalanches are commonplace on many mountains we have climbed, but they are not something you ever fully get used to, especially when you're sleeping. You hear them roar in the distance, jarring you out of your slumber. You're snapped wide-awake, your senses keen as you listen closely to judge their distance. Growing up in California, we're certainly used to an occasional earthquake and the unsettled feeling it brings as you wait for it to pass and wonder if it's going to be a strong one. We're just not used to them occurring every day and night like these avalanches. Many of them seem to go on forever; it feels like five minutes but in actuality, it's probably 30 seconds. Some of them are large enough and long enough to blanket our camp with a fine layer of "fallout" snow. We knew that our tents were deliberately set out of harm's way, but it was disconcerting nonetheless, particularly considering Heidi was killed by an avalanche only two weeks prior. We stayed still in our sleeping bags, listening, our heartbeats speeding up a bit before we settled back to sleep.

The mornings greeted us with small snowflakes falling from the inside walls of our tent, having accumulated through the night as hoarfrost. The inside of a tent is much like the inside of a car on a cold day. We were, in a sense, "fogging up the windows" with our breath through the night. Because of the below freezing temperatures both outside and inside the tent, this moisture transforms into a wall of ice crystals. Waking up each morning is therefore like waking up inside of the freezer compartments in the supermarket next to the frozen entrees and bags of frozen peas that have been coated with a thick layer of frost.

Also, if we neglected to put our water, toothpaste, sunscreen, etc. inside our sleeping bags with us before going to bed at night, they would end up frozen solid by morning. With the layer of hoarfrost on the ceiling and walls, it takes careful maneuvering not to set off a mini-snowstorm inside the tent during the morning routine.

Our next few days were spent acclimatizing to 17,500 feet and getting organized for the days ahead. I marveled at how difficult it was for me to pick up and carry the same duffle bag of gear that I could easily hoist and toss around just ten days ago, before coming up to this altitude. It was like being Superman under the crippling effects of Kryptonite. We looked forward to adjusting physiologically to the altitude and then heading up through the Icefall on our way to Camps 1 and 2. But first we had to wait for the all-important Puja ceremony.

A Puja is always held before a climb, and must be performed by a Lama. During the Puja ritual, the climbers and Sherpas pray to the gods for their permission to climb Mt. Everest and ask for blessings for a safe and successful expedition. Until this ceremony is held, no climber or Sherpa proceeds up the mountain for fear of angering the gods. Most expedition teams must arrange to have a Lama brought in from a village or monastery lower down in the valley in order to perform the ceremony. Our team was unique in that we had not only one but two full-fledged Lamas who happened to be part of our Sherpa staff. Dawa Geljen Sherpa was the sirdar in charge of our entire Sherpa team, and our cook Purba Surki, were both bona fide spiritually enlightened Buddhist Lamas. Despite the convenience of having two of our very own Lamas available to perform the Puja whenever it best fit into our schedule, this was not in the cards. Our Puja was re-scheduled for three days later than originally planned because, according to Dawa, that was deemed the proper timeframe for the spiritual satisfaction of the gods.

After the Puja ceremony, we would head to Camps 1 and 2 to begin our first acclimatization rotation. It is of utmost importance to make sure our bodies adjust properly to the increasingly higher altitudes so as not to jeopardize our quest for the summit, not to mention jeopardizing our lives. Because the Puja ceremony had been delayed, our plan to be back in time to see our Everybody to Everest team was in jeopardy. After all of our months of planning, it was difficult to grasp that a small change in schedule would alter everything we had worked so hard to organize.

The funny thing about living in a world so scheduled is that here on the greatest mountain on earth, things are also scheduled. But the difference is, that schedule is solely driven by the weather and a higher power. Our Puja ceremony had to wait because Dawa Sherpa said the days leading up would not be spiritually pleasing. We were now faced with a significant conflict between our carefully orchestrated plan and some sort of spiritual agenda we couldn't understand. On the one hand we have Scott, our expedition leader, who needs to get our team up the mountain to begin acclimatizing, and sticking to an important climbing schedule. On the other hand we have Dawa, conferring with the gods of the mountain, saying it's not time to go yet. Whom do you trust? I guess that depends on your level of spirituality. With a certain amount of reluctance we accepted the fact that this is a part of the Sherpa culture and their belief system, so although we may not fully comprehend, we needed to respect their beliefs and follow their spirituality when in their home. Scott was motivated to get us started to successfully make the summit, and we were similarly motivated to stick to the schedule to successfully greet our Everybody to Everest group when they arrived at Base Camp. Dawa was motivated to keep us safe and please the gods.

There are dissenting opinions as to the cause of the tragedy written about in "Into Thin Air." One of many contributing factors cited relates to a delayed Puja Ceremony. The Lama who was to perform the Puja didn't arrive at Base Camp on the planned date and the anxious leaders of the American climbing teams made a decision to proceed up the mountain through the Icefall prior to holding the ceremony. Ultimately their climb was a tragic one, claiming eight lives in one day and fifteen that 1996 season. Whether or not there was a correlation between the gods being angered by the disregarded timing of the Puja ceremony and the tragic events that later unfolded, is a matter of opinion. But that year was the single deadliest year in Everest history. One thing we do know is that the Sherpa people firmly believed it was bad luck to proceed without proper spiritual permission, and therefore their confidence and actions on the mountain were likely impacted. We were not going to take that chance, and furthermore respected the decision of Dawa to hold the Puja on the auspicious day he deemed appropriate. All we could do was hope the arrival of our Everybody to Everest group would coincide with our return from our five-day acclimatization trip to Camps 1 and 2.

While waiting for our Puja ceremony day to arrive, we did some training hikes to continue adjusting to the altitude. One of our hikes was to Kala Patthar, which lies beneath the south face of Pumori. Kala Patthar is a popular trek because it provides an accessible point to view Mt. Everest, since the peak itself cannot be seen from Everest Base Camp. We reached the high point, and stood in full view of our massive journey ahead. We weren't ready yet, but we would be very soon. It was exhilarating to see exactly where we were headed. We took a few photos and sat down gazing at the mountain, trying to absorb the significance of the task ahead and the inner strength and faith that would be required of us.

*View of Mt. Everest & Everest Base Camp from Kala Patthar*

Then it was finally time for the all-anticipated Puja ceremony. Prayer flags criss-crossed the camp: blue, white, red, green and yellow— symbolizing space, air, fire, water and earth. It is said that as the prayer flags move with the wind, the air is cleared, the earth is calmed, and their inscriptions release prayers to the heavens. We brought our crampons, ice axes and climbing harnesses up to the stupa and laid them upon the altar to be blessed. They were each individually adorned with a small amount of Yak butter to purify and protect this important climbing equipment that would in turn be protecting us. Dawa Geljen Sherpa and Purba Surki Sherpa performed the Puja, which lasted for half of the day and consisted of chantings from holy books and offerings of food (snacks, fruit, wine, beer, whiskey and cola) to the gods.

Unbeknownst to us, the offerings of food and drink were not intended entirely for the gods, and at the appropriate time during the ceremony, the food and drinks were passed around for all to enjoy. The whiskey and beer made several rounds through the audience with many takers. Denise and I refrained knowing we had an important climb through the Icefall the next day, and we only accepted a small amount of wine to be polite. We had previously learned the spiritual significance of the number three, symbolizing the three pillars of the Buddha, the Dharma (his teachings), and the Sangha (monks and nuns) and how many of the Sherpa traditions require things to be done in threes. The Sherpas took this ritual practice to heart, especially when pouring three whiskey shots! After all the prayers and blessings were recited and cel-ebrations concluded, we all threw rice into the air and smeared flour upon one another's faces symbolizing a hope that we may see each other when we are old and gray.

*Puja Ceremony – tossing rice into the air*

With our blessing now complete, it was time to prepare for the next steps in our journey—climbing up through the Khumbu Icefall.

• • • • •

————— *Step to the Summit* —————
## HAVE A LITTLE FAITH

Gazing up at spectacular Himalayan peaks or any mountain, forest, waterfall, or other natural beauty provides an ever-present reminder of the hand of a higher power in their creation. Many times in business and in life we get caught up in our efforts to control the physical world around us. And many times we actually feel successful in accomplishing this, thus perpetuating the myth that we alone have the power and are in control. We work hard, we make a plan and set a schedule; we achieve our goals, we generate profits in our business—WE are in CONTROL. But are we really? When staring up at the immense enormity of a mountain like Everest, and watching the storm clouds that form around her or the avalanches that come crashing down her slopes, it is foolishly delusional to think you are in control.

God, or whichever higher power you may believe in, is the one who is really in control here. The Sherpas know this and perform an elaborate Puja ceremony to acknowledge this omnipresent power. I believe having a strong sense of faith is what will carry you through the difficult and sometimes dangerous situations in life.

Even when making critical decisions in business, committing large amounts of capital, or otherwise taking significant risk, faith is a major factor. The overwhelming majority of my highly successful business owner clients give significant credit for their extraordinary success, to their faith in a higher power. It equips you with the con-

> *"No matter how steep the mountain—the Lord is going to climb it with you."*
> *—Helen Steiner Rice*

fidence to do more and be more knowing that God is on your side and with you every step of the way. Believing in oneself is certainly a prerequisite to achieving a certain level of success in everyday life. However, taking it one step higher by having strong faith and trust in God, and the ability to align your actions and purpose with His will, allows you to C.L.I.M.B. *(Step #2)* to a far higher level and reach more extraordinary summits of success and satisfaction than you may ever have dreamed.

*Our South Col Route – pioneered by*
*Edmund Hillary and Tenzing Norgay in 1953.*

*Map courtesy of www.alanarnette.com*
*© reproduction prohibited without authorization.*

---
*Step 9*
---

# MOVE FAST

*Create a personal imperative to complete high value / high priority tasks,
and move quickly to bring them to a conclusion.*

---

## CAUTION IN THE KHUMBU ICEFALL

Due to the exuberant celebration of some of the Sherpas during the Puja ceremony, our ascent through the Khumbu Icefall was delayed a day so they could have more time to organize their loads of gear and supplies for Camps 1 and 2. We tried to hide our disappointment as this was yet another hiccup in our schedule that could affect the greeting of our Everybody to Everest group the following week. So all that was left to do now was "have a little faith" that it would all work out. In the spirit of making the best use of our time, we used our extra day for a practice run part way through the Icefall.

It is imperative to go into the Icefall early in the morning during the coldest part of the day when the ice is most stable and least likely to collapse. We decided to load our packs to simulate exactly what we would be taking up on our first rotation to Camps 1 and 2. They seemed incredibly heavy. The plan was to hike until 10 a.m. at the latest, (before it got too warm in the Icefall) which would enable us to go about ¼ of the way through to reach the first aluminum ladder and practice getting across the crevasses with our crampons straddling the rungs. Our movements had to be very deliberate, carefully placing our boots and crampon points on the rungs. Denise had to be particularly attentive because she has a much smaller foot, wearing the equivalent of a men's size 8 climbing boot. Therefore she had to be even more precise making sure that the 1½ inch-long steel front points on each crampon were securely placed before taking a step.

I had a brief scare when I watched a climber from another team who appeared a bit careless with his steps. His crampons weren't securely positioned and sure enough, he took a frightful tumble. Fortunately he landed straight down onto the ladder straddling the rungs, and not over the edge! Shortly after witnessing this close call it was our turn to make this intimidating traverse. Denise was up first. I checked to make sure that her GoPro helmet cam was in position and recording, and off she went.

This was just a sampling of the huge task we would be embarking on the next day when we would pass all the way through the Icefall. We headed back to Base Camp for some rest and to get ready for our trip up to Camp 1.

*Denise crossing large crevasse in Khumbu Icefall. Photo by Scott Woolums*

The night before our first climb all the way through the Khumbu Icefall was a restless one. Denise and I felt like kids trying to sleep on Christmas Eve, tossing and turning and anxiously awaiting the day ahead. At 2:45 a.m. the alarm went off and we crawled out of our toasty sleeping bags and frosty tent into the frigid air. Before leaving we had another Buddhist ritual to perform. We circled three times (that important number three again) around the Puja stupa, burning juniper boughs and throwing rice. This was a reminder of ever-present danger and the importance of having faith on our journey. We were wearing the sacred necklaces given to us earlier by Lama Geshe from the village of Upper Pangboche. They were intended to protect us and we had no intention of taking them off considering where we were headed. At 4:15 a.m. we took one last look at the relatively comfortable and safe place we had called home for the last seven days and we made our way up into the Icefall.

The Khumbu Icefall is a bit like Disneyland combined with the heart-pounding anticipation of a horror movie. You are fascinated by its magic, but then you are almost waiting for something terrifying to happen. The Icefall is essentially an accumulation of glacial snow and ice from the upper parts of the mountain that is continually being deposited over what amounts to a cliff. It's a slow-moving frozen waterfall. It looks like a winter wonderland—artistic carvings out of an enormous block of cheese. However, this magical, gorgeous block of cheese can swallow you whole. I guess this is the one occasion in life where the cheese has one up on the mice.

> *"Life is either a daring adventure or nothing."*
> *—Helen Keller*

*The labyrinth in the Khumbu Icefall*

Our practice run the day before with our fully loaded packs turned out to be a beneficial one. As others struggled a bit, we were better prepared, having previously carried the same weight on our backs. Our steps were methodical, strategically placing our boots as we crossed over the multiple crevasses. I counted at least twenty crossings like this— some of the larger chasms had four aluminum ladders lashed together. The midpoint on these longer traverses, the point when anxiety was greatest, tended to cause these improvised bridges to bounce with each step, dipping down towards cavernous darkness below. My pulse quickened; my one encounter with a crevasse on Denali was enough, thank you very much. I did not want to experience that again.

Meanwhile, time was of the essence. With each passing hour the sun crept its way above the giant Himalayan peaks, its rays warming our shoulders and thawing our bodies from the chill of the pre-dawn hours. While this was a welcome feeling on our bodies, we knew the warmth of the sun would also cause the ice to melt and create dangerous instability.

Seracs, or blocks of ice, range in size from small cars to ten story office buildings. They can and do topple without notice, crushing climbers like a soda can under the force of a heavy boot. Simultaneously, as the minute hand sweeps around the clock during the daylight hours, the snowpack high above the Icefall on the face of Everest's West Shoulder becomes more susceptible to avalanches. There is now an additional danger of becoming buried by literally tens of thousands of pounds of snow and ice that could come crashing down while climbers below are navigating their way through the labyrinth of seracs, crevasses and ladders. While we were on the mountain a well-known Hungarian climber by the name of Laszlo Varkonyii met his maker in this tragic way. A small serac in the middle section of the North Col route collapsed sending down ice debris, striking the climbers on their fixed ropes. One was injured and evacuated but Varkonyii was swept down the slope into a deep crevasse. We were well aware of this ever-present danger of avalanches, the collapsing seracs, and the amount of time it took to make our way through this veritable death chamber.

Besides caution, the key word in reference to the Khumbu Icefall is time. There is a simple mathematical equation every Everest climber knows well. For each additional minute or hour spent in the Icefall, the probability of a dangerous occurrence increases proportionally. It is for this reason more Sherpas perish in the Icefall than Western climbers. The Sherpas are carrying more loads through and spending time setting up the ladders and then setting them up again after seracs inevitably topple over, hopefully while nobody is walking across that ladder. In fact, more climbers die in the Icefall than any other single part of the mountain.

Fortunately we moved fast and reached the top of the Icefall before 10:00 a.m. as Scott had hoped and planned. It wasn't long after we safely passed across the last set of ladders that one of those precariously perched seracs did in fact collapse. It destroyed the ladders and cut off the route for anybody else wanting to go up or down. Thankfully nobody was seriously hurt. Our prayers had been answered; we survived the first round of Russian roulette in the Khumbu Icefall. There would be five more trips necessary through this dangerous maze before the end of this expedition. This is simply what's required in order to physiologically prepare our bodies to function and survive in the altitude.

The effects of high altitude on humans are considerable. Our bodies function best at sea level. Hemoglobin is the protein molecule in red blood cells that carries oxygen from the lungs to the body's tissues and then returns carbon dioxide from the tissues to the lungs. After our bodies reach around 7,000 feet above sea level, the saturation of that protein in our blood cells begins to plummet. But our bodies are smart—they have both short-term and long-term adaptations to altitude to compensate for the lack of oxygen. Stressing the body for periods of time at high altitude triggers a long-term physiological adaptation for additional oxygen-carrying red blood cells to be created. They are produced in the bone marrow through a process called erythropoiesis. However this process takes time and requires rest and proper nutrition to be most effective. It's amazing to think that with each step higher, our bodies are constantly adjusting in attempts to protect us. All along the way we were measuring these adaptations with a pulse oximeter, an instrument similar to the one the doctors used earlier to diagnose the German woman near Tengboche. Knowing that our blood oxygen saturation levels were within an acceptable range as we ascended in altitude was comforting.

We would be spending two nights at Camp 1 at 20,000 feet. Camp 1 is quite exposed and much more windy than Base Camp. I didn't feel well at all. The altitude had finally caught up with me. I usually manage pretty flawlessly at this level, but this time I had severe nausea and an extreme loss of appetite. Denise encouraged me to eat, because without the necessary nutrients I would never make it another 1,500 feet to Camp 2. Neither of us slept well, both restless as the wind violently shook the walls of our tent. I reminded myself that acclimatization takes time and that I needed to have the patience to allow the physiological process to take place.

The next day we pushed onward through the Western Cwm (pronounced coom), also known as the Valley of Silence. The Western Cwm is a valley basin at the foot of the Lhotse Face. It was named by

George Mallory in 1921—thus its name, cwm that stands for bowl in Welsh. The central section is riddled with extensive lateral crevasses. Because of the radiant heat reflecting off of Nuptse to the East and the West Shoulder in a parabolic manner, this section of the mountain can quite ironically reach unbearably hot temperatures. In addition, the topography of the area tends to prevent much cooling wind from blowing and causes climbers to melt like an ice cream cone dropped by a child onto a scorching sidewalk. Nonetheless, conditions can rapidly change on Everest and temperatures can drop 100°F in less than an hour.

We managed to make it up to Camp 2 at 21,500 feet in less than three hours, which is considered to be a respectable time especially since we hadn't yet adjusted to this altitude. I was still having a tough go of it, and every step felt as if my legs had been poured with lead. Camp 2 also known as Advanced Base Camp or ABC, was better equipped than Camp 1, so our three-day stay was a little more comfortable. One of the other climbers, Cindy, had developed a nasty cough and I was thankful that I didn't have that in addition to my unstable stomach. Our daily hikes seemed to help my body settle in, but I knew Denise was worried that I was still unable to get in all of my necessary calories. We didn't want to be faced with that difficult decision of only one of us being healthy and strong enough to go on to the summit. So all I could do was bide my time and wait for my body to catch up. Patience, patience.

After three days at Camp 2 we were overjoyed to head back to Base Camp to greet our Everybody to Everest group who would be arriving the same day. The alarm went off at 3:45 a.m.—and we missed it! Denise looked at her watch at 4:15 and we both bolted out of our bags (well, as much as you can "bolt" at 21,500 feet). Of all days to be late! There's that time thing again. We scrambled to gather our gear, get our climbing harnesses on, and make our way down to Camp 1. We grabbed our climbing helmets and headed back through the Khumbu Icefall, which started off with a fairly significant rappel down a vertical drop of more than three stories high. After unclipping our figure 8's and continuing down, we witnessed the carnage from the collapsed serac we narrowly missed climbing through on the way up just days before. The group of Sherpas known as the "Icefall Doctors" had quickly re-routed the path around the collapse allowing traffic to continue. It was this type of occurrence, or the possibility of a bad storm, that we feared could prevent us from being able to see our friends during their arrival and brief overnight stay at Base Camp.

Denise and I led the way along with Dawang Chhu Sherpa, almost the entire remaining route down the Icefall—which took less than five hours total from Camp 2. Clearly we were fueled by adrenaline to see our friends. I forgot all about my stomach while Denise and I raced into Base Camp not knowing whether our Everybody to Everest group would already be there waiting.

•••••

—————— *Step to the Summit* ——————
## MOVE FAST

There are 168 hours in a week. Those who get on and ahead in life are those who use their 168 hours more effectively than the rest. In my occupation as an investment banker I am quite fortunate to work closely with many exceptionally successful entrepreneurs. I have learned a tremendous amount from this elite group who have defied the odds and built companies worth tens of millions of dollars. One of the common traits among this group of high performers is their ability to move fast. They create a personal imperative to quickly complete high value / high priority tasks that will lead them to achievement of their important goals. When I am representing these individuals in the sale of their companies, their single most valuable asset, I share with them an important philosophy about the M&A business. It is the notion that "time kills all deals". And they understand the concept well. The longer a merger or acquisition transaction takes to complete, the more opportunities can arise causing it to fail. I have seen this proven true over and over throughout my career and always attempt to instill an urgency of time among the parties to reach the finish line of the deal.

Imagine being in the Khumbu Icefall… If you knew the chances of being crushed by a falling serac or avalanche increased with each passing moment, you would certainly hurry to get through there as fast as you could. In that situation you wouldn't procrastinate or become distracted by anything that would impede your progress toward your goal. Create that same urgency and move rapidly to accomplish your priority objec-tives, and those key tasks or steps that will lead you to your summit of success. Start early in the morning while the less ambitious are still in bed, and move swiftly. Just as with the Khumbu Icefall, each moment that passes increases the chances that your important goals in business and life may collapse and come crashing down, shattering into pieces.

> *"Defer no time, delays have dangerous ends."*
> *—William Shakespeare*

# TAKE A STEP BACK

*Make sure to stop periodically along your climb to look back and appreciate how far you have traveled. Take a moment to celebrate your progress and assess what's truly important.*

## A SIGHT FOR SORE EYES

"Do you see them? Are they here yet?" we asked one another. Arriving back at Base Camp we were relieved to see that our Everybody to Everest group had not yet arrived. We knew they would likely show up soon so we rushed to get ourselves cleaned up. We retrieved a bucket of semi-warm water from the Sherpas who were busy cooking, and we made our way to our makeshift shower tent. I did not want to hug 23 people having not showered for six days! Plus, I had been in the exact same clothing up at Camp 1 and Camp 2 for the last five days and knew I couldn't have smelled too appealing at that point. We scrambled into clean clothes, brushed our teeth and stood on a large rock platform outside the dome tent, our eyes focused on the long trail below waiting for that first blue Everybody to Everest team jacket and red cap to round the corner into Base Camp. A large Everybody to Everest banner was hanging prominently on the dome tent to welcome the group.

Off in the distance the first dot of blue and red appeared, and I excitedly watched the colors bouncing along the stream, the dots getting larger and closer. They were here! I felt my heart fill with joy as they slowly shuffled into camp, one by one, hugging us as they filed in. Each individual greeting was quite emotional, as the reality set in that they had actually reached Base Camp. All of the effort in coordinating training, fundraising and travel had come to fruition. They made it, every single one of them. They had successfully attained the goal we had set the year before. It was amazing to see the whole group of 23 together. They had purposely waited for the slowest members to catch up so they could enter as a united front, each and every one of them wearing their blue team jackets and red caps. What a glorious sight for sore eyes, one we had been longing to see with great anticipation.

It was also interesting to see how everyone was doing physically. Most were incredibly winded and it quickly reminded us how we had felt when we had hiked into Base Camp for the first time only a few weeks prior. We got a kick out of seeing our normally clean-shaven, well-groomed friends looking like rugged mountain men and hippie chicks after weeks of roughing it. They may have looked tough on the outside, but it was obvious that their emotional inner side was bursting through. The joy and satisfaction of reaching their objective was written all over their faces, but what really hit me was what was evident in their eyes. Their eyes revealed a warmth and genuine affection towards us as friends, a feeling that was very much mutual. Some almost appeared to be holding back tears from the rush of overwhelming emotions intensifying inside of them. This special group of friends cared so much about us, they traveled to the other side of the globe and endured the struggle to reach us at this oxygen deficient altitude.

It was an amazing sight to see. Twenty-five of us from all walks of life, in matching jackets, filling the dome tent with animated voices and laughter. When the Everybody to Everest idea came to fruition, Denise and I weren't even sure anyone would want to go. Now to look around this oversized tent at all of these faces and think about

*"To look backward for a while is to refresh the eye, to restore it, and to render it more fit for its prime function of looking forward."*
*—Margaret Fairless Barber*

the achievements they had accomplished, it was difficult not to get choked up at the enormity of it all.

Another "participant" who made the journey half way around the world and all the way up the mountain to Base Camp was the "Sarah Bear." A cute stuffed teddy bear just like any other, except this one has a prosthetic leg. Sarah Reinertsen was the first female leg amputee to complete the Ironman Triathlon World Championship in Kona, Hawaii. She was born with a bone growth disorder that led her to becoming an above-the-knee amputee at the age of seven. After the amputation, and with the help of a prosthetic running leg, she began to run track and break records by the age of 13 and went on to compete in marathons, cycling races and triathlons. She is an inspiration to challenged and able-bodied athletes alike and her list of athletic accomplishments is lengthy. Sarah came up with the idea of distributing these teddy bears with a prosthetic leg to help kids cope with amputations and to understand that they are not alone. And that, like the bears, they are just as loveable even without an arm or leg. Before the trip, my sister Tina met with Sarah to pick up a Sarah Bear to bring along and everyone took turns carrying the bear up the mountain. It became an honor and a privilege to carry the bear. In fact, the Everybody to Everest group turned the daily handoff of the bear into a ceremony, explaining to whom they were passing it and why the chosen person should carry it next. The bear was a constant reminder of why we were all there and what we were there to accomplish.

We all had lunch together and a few people left the tent to wander over to the Icefall and get a closer look. Others found their tents and bags and took some time for a much-needed rest. We all gathered again in the dome tent, and as the warm day turned chilly, tea was passed around and everyone just chatted away. The sheer numbers of our group changed the face and character of our camp and the Sherpas did an amazing job taking care of everyone. I do appreciate how the members of our climbing team; Ania, Cindy, and Vivian, were such good sports and accepted this veritable invasion of so many outsiders into our camp. They quietly left the dome tent and retreated for some private time in their own tents. I couldn't mask my joy as I looked around the table at all of the excited (and tired) faces of our incredible friends. It was quite a surreal feeling and I tried to hang on to the moment for as long as I could.

The afternoon quickly turned to evening, the weather turned even colder and the snow continued to accumulate. One of our friends, Greg Hancock thought aloud, "Wow, this is the real deal." I think it had just hit him that he was sitting in a tent at 17,500 feet at the base of the highest mountain in the world. It was such a wonderful feeling to realize the significance of our friends' success. They had done what they came here to do. They had bought their gear, done their training and their fundraising, and made it all the way to Base Camp on Mt. Everest. At one point Greg jokingly said, "Hey, thanks for having us over to your place for dinner!" We all laughed and then I thought about the significance of that statement. C'mon over to our place for dinner—it will only take you 3 weeks, 17,500 feet of altitude, and thousands of dollars. Most people wouldn't drive in traffic across town for dinner. These 23 unbelievable people went to the other side of the world.

Our satiating meal was served by the very same Sherpas who had just earlier that day been all the way up at Camp 3 at 24,000 feet! Their strength and ability to accomplish so much never ceased to amaze me. Another friend of ours, Jeff Roberts, cranked up the music and we broke out into an all-out group sing-a-long, to the amusement of our climbing team and Sherpa staff who had poked their heads in the tent to witness 25 people singing at the top of their lungs. It was as if we had all been drinking up a storm at a bar, except for the fact that none of us had consumed a drop of alcohol. (Although later, our friend Shawn surprised us when he produced a bottle of expensive Cognac that he brought from home and carried all the way up for the entire group to share.) The singing and celebrations continued. I'm quite certain the volume level coming out of our camp that evening did not amuse the neighboring expedition camps of Peak Freaks and Alpine Ascents.

The next morning, we woke up early to do a live satellite phone interview with NBC News in Los Angeles. Our good friend Cindy Bertram had made these arrangements in advance, as a follow-up segment to a story about us that they filmed and aired on TV before we left home. We all shared a common goal to raise awareness for CAF and were thrilled about NBC's interest and enthusiasm for the story. We went inside the dome tent to connect the call and spoke to newscasters Chuck Henry and Colleen Williams live on the 5:00 evening news (factoring in the 12 hour and 45 minute time difference). It was strange to think we were actually speaking to a huge audience back home while they flashed photos of us on the screen, including several shots we had just taken at Base Camp with our entire Everybody to Everest group. They remarked on how clear our connection was and asked questions about the weather and how soon we would be heading up to attempt the summit. They also asked about the dangers involved in what we were doing and Denise responded to reassure Chuck and Colleen, as well our family and friends watching back home, that we would be fine. They wished us luck and told us they would be talking to us again soon. I hung up the phone and thought how cool that was... We were on the other side of the world, at an altitude of 17,500 feet, on top of a moving glacier, talking to the people in our home town, while they looked at pictures of us that were just taken the day prior. You've got to love modern technology.

It was about 6:30 in the morning when we finished the call, and folks were beginning to wake up and make their way to the dome tent for coffee and tea. Nobody had a truly restful night of sleep, considering the effects of altitude and the frequent sounds of avalanches with which we had become familiar. A few members of the group weren't feeling so well either. Branden was suffering from fairly debilitating stomach issues, Lou and Mike had evidence of edema in their faces, and my niece Stacie was also battling her stomach. All was a reminder that these were regular people with everyday lives attempting something beyond the comfort zone to which they were accustomed. And each of them seemed to experience their own personal moments of realization with the mountain.

My niece Stacie mentioned that she had gotten up in the middle of the night, climbed out of her tent, crawled over snow-covered rocks, vomited, and then looked up at the moon shining on the Khumbu Icefall and immediately forgot about her stomach. She was in awe of the beauty of this natural wonder. In spite of her difficulties at the moment, she decided to take a metaphorical step back to appreciate this astonishing faraway place to which she had hiked. Unbeknownst to Stacie or any of us at the time, back at home at nearly this exact moment, her mother Sonja had unexpectedly lost her battle with lung cancer and had just passed away. In the days before, while her health was rapidly deteriorating, my brother Mike desperately wanted to notify Stacie by satellite phone. But Sonja had insisted that nothing interfere with Stacie completing her Himalayan adventure, not even this. Perhaps however there was some cosmic/spiritual force trying to communicate to Stacie, as she gazed upon the moonlit icefall, to appreciate the beauty of this world and the beautiful life of her mother whose time on this Earth had just come to an end.

After breakfast, Dawa was busy setting up for a special Puja ceremony that would be performed for the Everybody to Everest group. The group gathered around the stupa with awesome views of the Icefall and surrounding peaks. Much like the first Puja, we gave offerings of money, beer and food. At one point during the ceremony, the clear blue skies gave way to a unique atmospheric phenomenon known as a parhelion, producing a spectacularly bright halo around the sun. These "sun dogs" as they are called, form when tiny hexagonal ice crystals in the air refract light at a precise 22° angle. The halo, with Everest as a backdrop and colorful strings of prayer flags flying overhead, provided an amazing photo from underneath the stupa. In fact, Dawa even stopped his ceremonial Buddhist chantings to take a photo for himself with his own camera! It was as if the Gods and angels in the heavens knew what we were doing and they were smiling upon us and offering their blessings at that very moment. In retrospect I cannot help but wonder if Stacie's mom was among those angels showing us a sign of her approval from above, letting us know that everything would be okay.

After the official ceremony ended, I felt a pit in my stomach as I realized it was now time for the Everybody to Everest group to gather their belongings and prepare to leave. We took individual photos with everyone by the stupa, and said emotional goodbyes as we wished them a safe journey back down the mountain, and they subsequently wished us a safe journey up. Denise and I stood on that same rock holding each other with tears in our eyes and watching sadly as they filtered out one by one. We stood there until the last speck of blue disappeared on the trail below.

I like to think that during our journey to Everest, we made an impact on the lives of these 23 friends who joined us on the adventure. And collectively we all made an impact on countless others who benefitted from the charitable contributions to CAF. This is what we came here to accomplish, and in many respects it was here at 17,500 feet, standing on a large rock outside of the dome tent, that we reached our summit.

• • • • •

*Step to the Summit*
# TAKE A STEP BACK

Just as coming back down to lower altitudes allows your body to recover and aid in the acclimatization process, it is also helpful for us in life to periodically take a moment to step back. It gives us an opportunity to celebrate and appreciate where we have been, and also to assess our progress and make necessary adjustments.

> *"Appreciation is a wonderful thing: It makes what is excellent in others belong to us as well."*
> *—Voltaire*

This gives us an opportunity to count our blessings and be thankful for our accomplishments and make sure to look at what is really important in life—whether it be family, friends and relationships, health and wellness, business and financial success, spiritual time and awareness, learning and growing, or fun and enjoyment. Be honest with yourself as you analyze how much quality time you are spending with each one. If some areas are lacking, taking that step back can help you to reprioritize your energy and make necessary course corrections in order to continue on the proper path to success.

Many years ago I heard somebody say that the true definition of success is "the progressive realization of a worthy goal or purpose." It's not necessarily the big house, career, big bank account, or even reaching the proverbial "top" as so many people believe. Success is the journey, it's the climb towards a meaningful goal and positively impacting lives. And you must take steps up towards that goal and make progress each and every day.

In order to help remember this, I came up with an acronym for S.U.M.M.I.T. = **S**uccess **U**ltimately **M**eans **M**aking an **I**mpact **T**oday.

It is my genuine hope that you will take the steps necessary to make an important impact in your own life by working towards your own meaningful goals. Along the way, through your thoughts, actions, priorities, and decisions, I wish that you positively impact as many lives as you are humanly able. Do this **T**oday, tomorrow, and every day. Take a step back to reflect as needed, and then continue your climb to the SUMMIT!

# MAINTAIN A SHARP FOCUS

*Concentrate your core energies and block out all distractions
that interfere with reaching your target.*

## IT'S A SLIPPERY SLOPE

There was an incredible quiet in camp once all of our friends departed after an emotionally charged 24 hours. I reflected proudly on what they had accomplished for CAF, for us, and especially for themselves. There was a strange emptiness after they left, similar to the day after a big wedding celebration. All of the guests had gone home and the bride and groom would sit reminiscing about all the events of the previous night while shifting into a new reality of everyday life. Only in this instance, our everyday life consisted of my bride and me washing dirty clothes in an icy stream and preparing for yet another trip up through the Khumbu Icefall for our second rotation, this time up to Camp 3 at 24,000 feet. It was snowing again, so we hung our clothes on a make-shift clothesline inside our tent to help them dry.

With the Everybody to Everest visit behind us, we now shifted our focus to the rest of our journey. Our now familiar routine of waking at 2:45 a.m. to have breakfast and depart for the high camps was back in motion. We made our ceremonial three circles around the stupa and headed into the Icefall. Our group seemed much more efficient this

> *"You must remain focused on your journey to greatness."*
> **—Les Brown**

time, with less hesitation at the ladders. This time after passing through the Icefall we stopped only briefly at Camp 1 to snack on a few Clif Bars before continuing. However, it was like somebody had cranked up the oven—the heat in the Western Cwm was unbearable and I slowly felt my energy diminish as we hiked the final steps up to Camp 2. We fared better than the rest of the group; perhaps it was because we had a sufficient amount of our electrolyte replacement drink, or maybe it was because we had an emotional re-charge from seeing our friends. Nonetheless, it was still ten hours total before we stumbled into Camp 2 and our familiar tent where we had left our sleeping bags and gear during the last rotation. We were parched and exhausted, but it wasn't long before one of our Sherpa staff came to bring us "juice" (which I think was hot Tang) and some ramen soup. That was exactly what our hungry, thirsty, sodium-depleted bodies craved the most! I will forever be grateful to the Sherpas for always taking such incredible care of us.

The next day was a scheduled rest day, which was a good thing not only because we needed it, but also because the weather was terrible. The winds at 21,500 feet can be fierce and it often felt like they would tear apart our tent. We leaned against opposite walls of the tent to keep it grounded. It felt like Dorothy's house in the "Wizard of Oz"—one big gust and we would go flying off the mountain. In fact, it is an all too common occurrence to lose tents in big wind storms at these higher camps. Before we left this camp on our first rotation, we took care to pack up all our belongings that we left behind (down suits, sleeping bags, summit mitts, etc.) even though they would stay behind in our tent. We couldn't take any chances of those fierce winds ripping open our tent and blowing our survival gear off the mountain. The margin for error is so thin in this environment. It's about as thin as the vinyl fabric of the walls of our tent providing a tenuous barrier between us and the bitterly cold, snowy, and unforgiving elements just outside. One wrong move or forgetful moment in caring for our gear, and the expedition could be over—or worse.

*Camp 2 typical harsh conditions at 21,500 feet*

It snowed most of the day but we did manage to brave the elements and go out for a brief walk after the winds died down. Sitting in a tent all day does not encourage the best acclimatization. Denise and I went out on our own and it was nice for us to be entirely alone for a bit in this vast and silent valley bordered by the steep slopes of Everest and Lhotse. We were still missing our friends, and besides we were hoping for a little quiet as Cindy's incessant coughing that had begun eight days prior was still persisting and proving to be quite distracting. Beyond the distraction of the continuous coughing day and night, we were worried about the health of one of the members of our team. Part of our frustration was a concern that perhaps Cindy could be doing more to treat the cough, as Bill and Scott had provided recommendations. Nonetheless, we did what we could and shared our supply of cough lozenges with her and tried to tune out the coughing and stay focused. For we had a formidable obstacle ahead of us in the days to come that would require complete focus—the Lhotse Face.

Lhotse stands at 27,940 feet and is the fourth highest mountain in the world after Everest, K2 and Kanchenjunga. Lhotse connects to Everest by way of the South Col (the highest camp before the summit), and is characterized by the extreme steepness of its face (2 miles vertical gain with only 1.4 miles of horizontal distance). We would be required to climb a good portion of it in order to reach Camp 3 and eventually the South Col. The weather was still unstable, so we took a hike just to the base instead of attempting to climb up the face. It ended up snowing the rest of the day and we spent our time in our tent, in our sleeping bags—a common pastime up at Camp 2. Conditions permitting, we would climb the Lhotse Face the next day.

Our goal was to reach Camp 3, a difficult 2,500 vertical feet above our current location at Camp 2. We were up at 3:45 a.m. for a 5 a.m. departure. The weather was still not ideal with a thin cloud layer blocking out the moon. By the time we reached the base and before starting up the fixed lines it was snowing and cold enough that we needed our goggles to keep our faces warm. We clipped our ascenders onto the fixed line and began to climb the steep and tricky bergschrund at the beginning. Once beyond this roughly 40-foot vertical obstacle, the climb was steep—steeper than any other slope we had climbed in our lives. And it went on and on relentlessly without a hint of a flat spot to be found anywhere. We were fortunate to be virtually the only team climbing at this time of the morning; our Sherpa team had left hours before us, carrying loads of oxygen cylinders, and were well above us already en route to the South Col.

We made steady progress and as we continued up, the views expanded and the valley (and Camp 2) seemed so far below us. It became abundantly clear to us at this point that losing focus and making one wrong move on this slope would be a death sentence. It would be like sliding 2,000 vertical feet down the equivalent of an ice skating rink tilted at a 55° to 65° angle. Surviving a fall like this is virtually impossible and those who have witnessed climbers experience this horrible end, describe a rag doll-like body tumbling and leaving a trail of blood in its path.

We maintained our concentration and took one step after another with labored breathing in the increasingly thin, oxygen-deficient air. Finally we made our way up to Camp 3 at 24,000 feet on the Lhotse Face. We kicked the heels of our crampons in for stability on the steep slope and collapsed on our packs to take a rest. This marked a major milestone for us, as it was now officially the highest altitude to which we had ever climbed. We were higher than all of the other Seven Summits at this point, even higher than the mighty Aconcagua in the Andes at 22,843 feet. I couldn't have imagined back then, after reaching that lofty summit in South America, what it would feel like to climb more than 1,000 vertical feet higher. Our hearts and lungs were already working overtime up here and thinking about our ultimate goal being almost an entire vertical mile above us was beyond comprehension. With our task of reaching Camp 3 now complete, the only thing for us to focus on was getting ourselves safely back down the Lhotse Face.

Descending the fixed lines was a bit tricky in places due to the steepness, so we used figure 8's to rappel occasionally, but mostly we used an arm-wrap technique around the rope as a way to control our descent. The friction caused my gloves to get quite hot at times but once we got into a rhythm and felt comfortable, the rappel went quickly particularly as compared to the climbers we encountered who were on their way up and seemed to be moving like statues.

Focus is incredibly important on the descents. A tired or careless climber can easily catch the spikes of his crampons on the opposite leg or boot and go tumbling head over tea kettle. I admit I was guilty of committing this blunder once or twice in my early days of mountaineering. This was not a place for a repeat of one of those moves. For this reason and for many others you don't have the luxury of letting your mind wander on a slope like this and at this altitude. Conversations with others are not substantive because the brain is not functioning at full capacity due to the lack of oxygen. You only have enough attention span to conduct the task at hand. In a sense that's really the fundamental beauty of climbing and enjoying certain outdoor adventures. You have no choice but to be in the moment. You don't have the ability to sweat the small stuff or even comprehend the big picture entirely. It's all about being focused and present.

We ended up back at Camp 2 around 1 p.m. and had a much-needed nourishing lunch and a nap. It was then that I realized I might have picked up some kind of cold bug as I was blowing my nose much more frequently and my head felt congested. We had been taking so many precautions with hygiene, but at this altitude and physical exertion level the immune system is constantly compromised. I hoped it would dissipate quickly. Denise was taking care of me quite well in our tent and braved the elements outside several times to bring soup and dinner back to me. Keep in mind that putting on your boots, getting up and out of the tent, carefully unzipping the door so as not to let in snow, going to the other tent to get food and bringing it back can be at least a 15-20 minute process at that altitude. I felt a little guilty about Denise having to go back and forth to care for me but we were trying to be considerate so as not to spread germs to others.

Fortunately the next day was a planned rest day at Camp 2 to recover from our climb of the Lhotse Face. Now Denise wasn't feeling very well either and had stomach issues that were really draining her energy. Luckily this hadn't appeared the day before or it would have made climbing to Camp 3 nearly impossible. She wasn't very interested in drinking water since it sometimes tasted a bit like kerosene, but it was my time to encourage her to hydrate and stay focused on her health. She drifted off to sleep and I took advantage of the down time to do a bit of reading.

The next day was another early morning rise to head down through the Icefall for our 4th trip, and back to Base Camp. I recall thinking that the next time we returned up here would be for our summit push! Luckily Denise and I were both feeling better.

It was an overcast morning, which turned into a light snow by the time we passed Camp 1 and started climbing down. We continued to worry about Cindy. Normally she had kept pace with the rest of the team, but today her persistent cough seemed to have zapped her energy and she fell a bit behind. Fortunately Bill was there to aid her along the way. Hopefully when we got back to lower altitude she could regain some of her strength.

It was a familiar treat returning to Base Camp and to our tent with all of our clean clothing and other conveniences. Surki of course had a brunch prepared for us, which was even more enjoyable to be eating back in our large, plush dome tent with comfortable chairs. During our meal we discussed the next step of our acclimatization program which would entail descending to a lower elevation than Base Camp for a few days. The additional oxygen there would give our bodies an opportunity to rest and recover from the strains we had been putting them through and regain the strength needed for the upcoming summit push. After Scott reviewed the weather forecast it was decided that we would head down to Dingboche the next day. This would give us three days of recuperation and allow enough time to return to Base Camp and prepare for a window of seemingly calm winds on the summit in just ten days. We were reluctant to leave Base Camp so soon but liked the idea of going down to Dingboche—for it meant we were one step closer to achieving our goal.

· · · · ·

## *Step to the Summit*
## MAINTAIN A SHARP FOCUS

Living in such a fast-paced world, it's easy to get distracted and lose focus in your daily life. Emails ding in your inbox, smartphones buzz in your pocket, text messages, tweets and Facebook notifications constantly blink to taunt you to stop what you are doing or thinking about in favor of paying attention to something else. And usually that something else is in no way related to helping you achieve your important goals. On

Everest our ever-present goal was to reach the summit and return safely. Fortunately we didn't have all of the distractions of electronics and the Internet to pull our attention away from our goal, but there were others. The persistent coughing of one of the members of our team was a seemingly small thing, but like technology interruptions, it was enough to serve as a mental pattern interrupt. We needed to block out these interferences in order to stay focused on our goal, and on our safety and survival.

> *"Concentrate all your thoughts on the work at hand. The sun's rays do not burn until brought to a focus."*
> *—Alexander Graham Bell*

The prefrontal cortex is the most evolved part of our brain and it serves an indispensible function in helping us reach our goals. In his book, "Change Your Brain, Change Your Life," psychiatrist and neuroscientist Daniel G. Amen discusses how to optimize brain function. The prefrontal cortex is involved with focus, concentration, and attention span. Dr. Amen says that having a clear idea of your goals strengthens this part of the brain guiding thoughts and behaviors. Giving your brain something positive as a goal (something you like and desire) also has immune system benefits, while negative thoughts and negative focus do the opposite.

So, maintain a sharp focus on the task at hand, don't allow outside distractions to pull you away from your important goals, and take your next step to success!

---
*Step 12*
---

# BUILD QUALITY
# RELATIONSHIPS

*Harness the power of personal relationships. You will enjoy the
climb and go much higher than you ever thought possible.*

---

## THE CLOTHES OFF OUR BACKS

We set aside our sleeping bags and clothing for the porters to carry, grabbed our daypacks and headed down towards Gorak Shep, Lobuche, and eventually Dingboche. It was a relief that we only needed to transport necessities for the day like fluids and extra layers of clothing. During the course of our expedition I was always so impressed by how piles of gear would magically appear at each destination; we would pack it up and leave it at camp, and then voila—it would be waiting for us at our next stop. The five-hour hike was actually a much needed rest day for us, and since the path was a familiar one, Denise and I decided to steal a little alone time. It often occurred to me on this trip that although I played a role as a member of a team achieving a common goal, I also had a role first and foremost as a husband. So when opportunities like this arose, we made sure to take advantage of the time to ourselves.

Physically, there was still something not quite right with my health. The congestion I had felt up at Camp 2 was lingering, and I was hopeful that the increased oxygen in Dingboche (14,250 feet) would cure all that ailed me. We passed a slow group of trekkers who were laboring in the altitude and it was nice to realize how far physically we had already come on this journey. This trip down to Dingboche would be the turning point. Our trek back up the mountain would be all the way to the top! The weather quickly turned bleak and the wind picked up. We grabbed warmer layers out of our packs and were overjoyed to eventually spot the faint outline of the Snow Lion Lodge peeking through the thick fog off in the distance.

Mingma greeted us with a big hug and promptly offered us her special room (the one we had previously dubbed "The Honeymoon Suite"). We were thrilled that she had made it available to us again, and looked forward to the porters arriving with our bags of fresh clothing and sleeping bags. More importantly, we looked forward to our first night out of a tent in weeks.

We relaxed in front of the yak dung-fueled heater in the dining room, along with a Columbian climbing team named Epopeya. Their expedition centered on Nelson Cardona, a below-knee amputee who lost his right leg while training to climb Everest in 2007. Outfitted with a specialized new leg from the prosthetic manufacturing company Ossur, Nelson was back to tackle the mountain. We were very proud to inform him why we were there; we told him all about CAF and the Everybody to Everest group. He was noticeably moved by our collective efforts to help injured individuals like him pursue their dreams and live life to the fullest. We chatted for quite a while and later took a photo together, promising to look for each other during the push to the summit. I couldn't help but feel an enormous sense of pride to be able to meet this challenged athlete and share in this amazing journey.

There was also another group of trekkers from Arizona who overheard our chat with Nelson and mentioned that they had recently made a donation to CAF as well. It was as if all of the CAF athletes back home had unknowingly sent us a little added inspiration clear across the world. Seeing Nelson Cardona's prosthetic leg propped up against a wall in a teahouse dining room in Dingboche was a poignant reminder of the bigger picture as to why I was even there to accomplish this immense conquest in the first place. It was yet another one of those "Pinch me" moments that I often had during this journey.

*With amputee Nelson Cardona – Team Epopeya, Columbia*

We lingered in the dining room of the Snow Lion Lodge and were beginning to get concerned that our sleeping bags and clothes had not yet arrived. I thought back to how often we had left things behind for the porters during the trip. We'd left gear collectively at Base Camp and Camp 2 just assuming it would be there the next time we returned. It occurred to me how many assumptions were made on the mountain. We were entrusting many aspects of our safety and survival to others. We relied on the Sherpas and porters, our guides and each other simply based on the confidence of the business and personal relationships formed. We had just assumed our bags would show up. It had happened every other time, why not this time? It's not like we could just send a text message to the porters asking their ETA. They could be anywhere, and now it was dark outside. The continuous ticking of the clock suggested to us that the sweaty clothes clinging to our backs might be the only clothes we would have for this respite. We waited and waited, sipping tea and nervously chatting as the hours crept by. At 9 p.m. we accepted the fact that our belongings would definitely not be arriving at the lodge that night. We began discussing our options and whether there were any spare blankets available. If nothing else, at that point I was certainly thankful to have my wife to keep me warm.

Trying to make light of our situation, I thought it would be entertaining to pose a hypothetical question to the ladies of the group. "Which would you rather have if you could snap your fingers and instantly make one or the other appear: your husband/boyfriend or your sleeping bag?" Cindy answered first. She hesitated a brief moment and then made it clear there would really be no question. Her reply: "My sleeping bag." Ania's response was even more emphatic: "I would choose my sleeping bag of course." Their answers were incredibly surprising to me, shocking really. Without a doubt my answer would have been Denise, and hers would have been me. What was crystal clear to me at that moment was something I had known all along; I would not have wanted to complete this life-altering journey climbing the Seven Summits any other way than with Denise by my side for every step of the process. I felt so fortunate and truly blessed to have the opportunity to share this unique adventure with her. Our marriage was being cultivated and strengthened with every footprint we left in the snow. Mingma returned with a pile of blankets and although we didn't have our personal belongings, we happily made use of our collective body heat back in our Honeymoon Suite and drifted off to sleep.

> *"The quality of your life is the quality of your relationships."*
> *—Anthony Robbins*

The next day was a welcome relaxation day in Dingboche. Our bags had finally arrived and we were elated to change into warmer clothes. Mingma went to great lengths to fill our bellies with wonderful food like apple pancakes and stir fried noodles with fried eggs. Our appetites had noticeably increased down at the lower elevation and we took the opportunity to eat to our heart's content. We had lots of fun calling Mingma our stand-in Sherpa mom, and appropriately it was Mother's Day weekend. It had been more than a month now since we had left my mom's house for the airport on Easter Sunday. We had prearranged to send flowers to both of our moms; this was the first Mother's Day in a long time that we had not been able to see them. It was strange to think we had been on this mountain for so many weeks, with life continuing as normal back home. Our families and friends were going about their typical routines, and business was still carrying on back at the office. We did our best to stay in touch, but had no control over the continuance of life while we were so far away.

We had been updating our blog, "Seven Summits for CAF" along the way, and took the opportunity to head to the Internet café at the upper end of Dingboche to make a post wishing our moms and all of the other moms who were following along, a happy Mother's Day. We also created a fun list to post on that blog entry called "The Top Ten Things We Miss The Most." And here are the winners:

1.) *A shower*
2.) *Clean clothes*
3.) *A bed*
4.) *A toilet —other than hole in ground or "wag bag"*
5.) *Fresh fruit / salad*
6.) *Water from a faucet*
7.) *A "bedroom" that is larger than 6 feet x 4 feet*
8.) *Oxygen… and the ability to do the following without gasping for air:*
   *– Get dressed in the morning*
   *– Brush teeth*
   *– Tie shoes*
   *– Go to the bathroom*
9.) *Sleeping without being woken up several times by the sound of an avalanche*
10.) *The ability to get out of our non-existent bed (see #3) and walk out of our spacious bedroom (see #7) without first putting on eight layers of cloth-ing (see #2) and not gasping for air while blazing a trail through the snow without the need of a headlamp, all just to go to the bathroom (see #4)!*

After returning to the Snow Lion Lodge, we noticed our climbing team sitting in the courtyard chatting with a man we didn't recognize. I was pleased to discover that the man turned out to be the famous high altitude researcher and "Everest ER Doctor" Peter Hackett. Dr. Hackett is extremely well respected in mountaineering circles for his vast knowledge on high altitude physiology. Upon graduating from medical school, he was first employed as a helicopter rescue doctor in Yosemite National Park. His love of mountain rescue led him to Nepal and he climbed Mt. Everest in 1981. He researched his way to the summit, recording his own health changes and gathering data for his studies. He had a close call on his descent, nearly dying from a fall on the Hillary Step. Dr. Hackett was heavily involved in starting the Himalayan Rescue Association, currently with two clinics in Nepal. He is also the founder of the Wilderness Medical Society and is the Executive Director of the Institute for Altitude Medicine, located in Telluride, Colorado.

Our guides Scott and Bill have known Dr. Hackett for many years, and thanks to that relationship we had an inside track to this great resource. We sat down to enjoy lunch with Dr. Hackett, and ended up having a fascinating medical discussion at the same time. He was also pleased to receive a special greeting we had to pass along to him. Our family physician back at home in California, Dr. Janet Goodfellow, knew Peter well through one of his associates. We learned of this relationship when we met with Dr. Goodfellow in order to have some prescriptions filled for emergency high altitude medications, and to have her sign a medical release form for us. When you commit to climbing to such high elevations as Everest, guiding companies like Mountain Trip and others require that you provide physician signed medical forms stating that you are physically fit enough to make the ascent. We had gotten into a discussion with Dr. Goodfellow about all of the advances made in the study of high altitude physiology, and much of that body of knowledge can be attributed to research done by Dr. Hackett.

Surprisingly, one of the drugs on our list of emergency medications was Viagra. At first I didn't know whether this was some kind of a joke, or perhaps a misprint. For our own health and safety I knew that we would be required to perform physiologically at high altitude, but not perform in *this* way! Maybe the guys at Mountain Trip were just trying to be helpful knowing that this would be a long two months on the mountain for husband and wife climbing partners? After a bit of a chuckle with Dr. Goodfellow, she explained that Viagra is a vasodilator. Vasodilation means an increase in the size of blood vessels. When you're up at high elevation, your blood vessels can constrict causing normal blood flow to vital organs to decrease. So having a drug such as Viagra on hand can be quite beneficial up at the higher altitudes in case of an emergency. I just wasn't sure which vital organs we were trying to protect here!

Another useful drug is dexamethasone. Often referred to simply as "Dex", this is a powerful steroid used as an anti-inflammatory and immunosuppressant. It is often utilized as treatment of rheumatoid arthritis but at high elevation has proven to be extremely helpful in cases of cerebral and pulmonary edema.

We talked at length with Dr. Hackett about how these drugs have improved the chances of survival in many life and death situations high up on Everest and other big peaks. We recalled the dramatic rescue of the German climber that we witnessed on Denali after he was injected with Dex, which ultimately helped save his life. Another interesting subject Dr. Hackett brought up was the noticeably faster speed in which cells regenerate down at lower elevations. I had a small cut on my thumb for over two weeks that simply wouldn't heal up at Camp 2 or at Base Camp. But now with the additional oxygen at this lower elevation, I noticed it was finally starting to get better. It was fascinating to be able to sit with this doctor and hear tales of his adventures on the mountain. It was clear the relationships he had formed with the Sherpa people were beneficial not only to the community but to the hundreds of climbers each year who passed through as well.

After lunch we decided to take a much-needed shower and spend some alone time back in the Honeymoon Suite. All of the emergency medications, including the blue pills, stayed in their protective packaging. I must say, I think Ania and Cindy were wrong in choosing their sleeping bags over their significant others.

The next morning, we had mixed emotions as we left Mingma

115

and the Snow Lion Lodge to head back up to Lobuche and eventually on to Base Camp. We had really enjoyed our brief three-day "low-altitude vacation" and Mingma's hospitality, and had a great time meeting Nelson Cardona and Dr. Hackett. Leaving the Snow Lion Lodge also meant one more thing; our final journey to the summit had begun. We left our bags with the porters and set out on the path.

• • • • •

—————— *Step to the Summit* ——————
## BUILD QUALITY RELATIONSHIPS

It is an undeniable fact that in business, relationships are key to success. Whether you're climbing the corporate ladder, an aluminum ladder in the Khumbu Icefall, or creating the next entrepreneurial success story, you simply cannot go it alone. Invest time cultivating relationships built upon trust. Establish rapport with those who care about your success and well being as much as you genuinely care about theirs, and you will form a launching pad to propel you anywhere you want to go in business and in life.

> *"Personal relationships are the fertile soil from which all advancement, all success, all achievement in life grows."*
> —Ben Stein

Climbing big mountains in business and in life requires meaningful communication and partnering with the right individuals, at the right time along the way. On Everest, our relationships with our

116

guides, Sherpas, climbing partners and others with whom we interfaced were effective and based on mutual respect. The same was true among our Sherpa team, many of whom had worked together on the mountain for many seasons. A good number of them were related by family in some way, and those who weren't, still referred to one another as "brother." The connections and relationships our guides had built and nurtured over the years with the Sherpas and other key individuals were imperative building blocks allowing us to achieve our goals. We deeply respected these relationships and considered it our responsibility to build upon them further. Just as the Sherpas were caring for our well being and success, we did what we could to care for theirs as well.

Selecting the right partners with whom to build these relationships is indeed critical. Evaluate chemistry, compatibility, and core values very carefully, and don't ignore your gut. This also holds true when selecting key employees or outside advisors to your business. Partnering with the right attorney, CPA and investment banker can have significant influence on the outcomes and strategic direction of your enterprise. Similarly the right choice of a business partner can make the difference between financial success and ruin, a partner in marriage can determine blissful contentment or despair, and the right choice of a climbing partner can make the difference between life and death.

Remember, regardless of your skill or expertise in your field, or your mastery of all of the other Steps to the Summit, without building quality relationships with the right partners, you simply cannot make it to the top. Nor can you expect to stay there.

# MAKE A DECISION

*Decisions determine success. Have the courage to make the*
*right decisions that will lead you to the top.*

## STOPPED COLD BY THE WIND

The sunshine seemed brighter this morning as if to illuminate the final path towards the goal we had been working so hard to achieve. After a few hours on the trail towards Lobuche, happily soaking up the sights of the jagged Himalayan peaks above and the meandering glacial-carved valleys below, our mood suddenly became somber. We had reached the sacred chorten monuments memorializing the more than 200 climbers who had died on the slopes of Everest. Although we had walked this consecrated land previously, this time was different. We would now be heading all the way up to where these climbers took their final steps in life, perhaps wishing they could go back and do things differently. It was as though I could hear their voices whispering from the stone piles telling me to choose wisely in the days ahead, there's a lot at stake here.

We continued on to Lobuche and the next day through Gorak Shep and back up to Base Camp. It was actually comforting to return to our home away from home. We were relieved to have all of our belongings in one place (except for the gear up at Camp 2) so we reorganized our things and made our way to the dome tent. It feels odd to say it was a relief to be back in the modern conveniences of the dome tent, but since Scott and Bill had it set up like a virtual command center, part of me felt like I was back at the office. The only difference was that this office was at an altitude of 17,500 feet and had a cook named Purba Surki preparing amazing meals for me.

Now that this journey was in the home stretch, it was time for Scott to do the final agonizing analysis of the weather. Successful summits of Everest can in many respects be largely attributed to picking the right days to go for the top. If the winds are too high, temperatures too cold, or there are heavy accumulations of snow, nobody will make it to the summit. There are only brief windows of remotely hospitable conditions on Everest each year. Those days typically occur sometime in May when the jet stream is temporarily pushed north due to pressure zones forming over the Bay of Bengal. Throughout the rest of the year, with the exception of short periods in October, the summit of Everest is constantly battered by powerful jet stream winds exceeding 150 miles per hour.

The decision-making process in picking this brief window of favorable weather can be an excruciating one, and I certainly didn't envy Scott's position. This single decision could be incredibly costly. He had an entire team who not only had paid a hefty sum for the trip itself, but were also relying solely on him for the green light to go for the summit. And relying on him to give that signal at the appropriate time. Achieving the coveted goal of making it to the top, in many ways rested in Scott's hands and in this one decision. Every single person here had put his or her life on hold for two months and a simple change of his mind could erase years of preparation.

> *"In any moment of decision the best thing you can do is the right thing, the next best thing is the wrong thing, and the worst thing you can do is nothing."*
> *—Theodore Roosevelt*

There are many different sources to research and compare when it comes to forecasting the weather on Everest. The NOAA—National Oceanic and Atmospheric Administration is a widely used resource. Its website has constant climate change updates and their scientific studies on environmental matters are unparalleled. Mountain Trip had also purchased several other Everest-specific weather forecast services providing us by e-mail every few days a dizzying array of colorful charts, graphs, and data that would make your typical scientist or engineer salivate. The reports showed trends and had specific predictions for temperature, wind velocity, and snowfall at various elevations all the way to the summit at over 29,000 feet. After digesting all of the data, it appeared as though there would be a brief window of lower winds (20-30 mph) six days away on May 17th. However on the days preceding and following, the winds were predicted to be significantly higher (70 mph) and therefore could be considered a risky time to make a summit attempt. The next feasible window was a whopping eleven days away on May 22nd.

That posed yet another concern because the monsoon season begins each year around the end of May. It is a period of intense storms and heavy snowfall making the climb to the summit virtually impossible. In addition, the warmer temperatures lower on the mountain around this time make the Khumbu Icefall even more dangerous and deadly than usual. A decision is made when the monsoon arrives, the Icefall Doctors are dispatched to remove all of the ladders from the route, and the mountain is effectively closed for the season. Last year this occurred on May 25th just days after the May 22nd date we were debating as an alternate summit window. This wouldn't leave much extra cushion.

The weather discussions were ongoing during the next few days and Scott involved us in the decision-making process. I assumed this was part of his leadership style and a means to share some ownership for the decision with us in case it turned out to be wrong. But after studying the forecasts myself and comparing them to forecasts from previous seasons that Scott had wisely archived for reference, it became obvious that this was a difficult decision for him and for everybody, with no clear answer. I felt my anxiety rise for the first time since commencing on this trek. Would it be too risky to go for the shorter window on the 17th? Would we miss our chance to even attempt the summit if we waited too long for the next window on the 22nd?

The word "forecast" quickly became the "F" word to us. We heard rumors of various teams heading up to Camp 2 to get in position for their summit attempt. We were paid a visit by Nobu, a Chinese-born real estate developer and friend we had made in Antarctica on our Vinson climb. He came by our tent to discuss the weather forecast in more detail with Scott. He had obtained an extensive weather report from China, which sounded like it contained some different data than ours. Nobu had made the decision to attempt the summit during the brief window on the 17th. He would be leaving Base Camp the next day on the 13th in order to get into position, as a few other teams were doing as well. Part of me felt like we should be going too. Ultimately though, we all came to the same conclusion that the margin of error was too thin to risk the shorter window on the 17th. As a consequence, if by waiting until the 22nd we missed our chance to even take a shot, we would certainly be devastated. But we valued life most, so it would be a decision we would live with.

We had another visitor during this time who left us with some sage advice. Her name was Valerie, a British friend of Scott's who was living in Nepal and Tibet, leading treks for five months out of the year. She told us the story of her recent Everest climb and how one of her team members, Mike, had the misfortune of suffering from snow blindness on the way to the summit. The condition is a temporary burn of the eye's cornea caused by ultraviolet B rays and often can occur at high altitudes. Valerie said a painstakingly slow decision about how to help their teammate and the decision to ultimately turn around, led to more injury for the group. While waiting in the bitter cold trying to figure out what to do, she suffered from severe frostbite on her toes. Following the aborted summit attempt she later learned, quite unfortunately, that she needed to have portions of her toes amputated. Valerie's advice to us was to keep moving at all costs on summit day in order to keep warm. I didn't take her words lightly—above anything else, our lives and limbs were more important than reaching the summit.

During our extra days in Base Camp waiting for the later summit window, we received some confirming feedback that we had made the right call in staying. The winds started howling through the valley like never before. I looked up at the ominous clouds and felt relieved to be in the safer confines of Base Camp rather than up high on the mountain.

The wind whipped through camp violently shaking the tents (and our nerves). Pinju Sherpa radioed down from his post at Camp 2 letting us know he was okay and that he had managed to collapse all of our tents there to prevent them from blowing away. I thought about all of the belongings we had left up there: our 40-below rated Marmot sleeping bags, down suits, gloves and summit gear. As the day went on, the radio chatter indicated that some teams at Camp 2 were abandoning their summit attempts and returning to Base Camp. There were already some teams who had reached Camp 3 and I said a silent prayer for their safe summit and return. Their success would also be a direct complement to ours; if more teams could summit early, then there would be less congestion on the route when the rest of the teams made an attempt during the next weather window on the 22nd.

It was imperative that we stay fit during this waiting period, so we hiked to Pumori Base Camp, about an hour and a half away. We ran into some acquaintances from home, a father and son team John and Ryan Dahlem, who were climbing with the well-respected guiding outfit International Mountain Guides (IMG). They told us about a body that had just been discovered in the Icefall by a waste clean-up team. It was an IMG Sherpa, a relative of some of their current Sherpa team members. He died in the Icefall back in 2006 and astonishingly his body was still intact. The Sherpas conveyed the news of this discovery to the widow and carried the body down to the village Pangboche for a cremation ceremony. This was yet another grim reminder of the dangers of what we were attempting, yet the Sherpas considered it a good omen that he was found because there is closure and the victim's spirit can be properly sent up into the heavens above. This was also another sign of the deep spirituality rooted in the mountain and the characteristics of its people.

The days waiting for the weather window were nothing short of monotonous; we filled our time doing training hikes to continue our constant acclimatization. During a hike up to the Pumori Camp 1 at 19,000 feet, we ran into longtime Everest guide Russell Brice and his team. He had become a bit of a celebrity due to his role in the Discovery Channel series, "Everest—Beyond The Limits." It was reassuring to see that he too, had decided to wait until the next bout of good weather. I couldn't help but have doubts in the back of my mind about the possibility that we had blown our chance to go for the summit; seeing that Russell had waited as well was comforting.

*With Russell Brice of Discovery Channel notoriety, at Pumori Camp 1*

News of groups reaching the summit began to trickle in. In the midst of constant weather discussion and rumors of other team's summit strategy, it was a challenge to keep our minds focused on the task at hand. I shifted my attention slightly to business going on back home and used the satellite phone to check in on my client, the owner of the large medical device company. My colleague was trying to help me get the deal back on track with another buyer. It was imperative that, while up on this mountain, I still maintained the relationships with my clients at home. Early in the evening Dr. Hackett came over from his Himalayan Rescue Association tent located in the "midtown" section of Base Camp, as we called it, to join us for dinner. It was wonderful to be able to continue our chat with him. I enjoyed learning more about high altitude medical developments and discussing my client's business and the impacts of U.S. Healthcare reform. And on a lighter note, I was quite amused to hear his stories of touring with the Rolling Stones as the band's medical doctor. What a gig that must have been.

The days crept by and the ice platform on which our tent rested began to melt and shift as the weather changed. Did we miss our window? We got word that Nelson Cardona had reached the summit and I felt another tremendous burst of pride that he had accomplished his goal after working so hard to come back from his prior accident and losing his leg. Then our good news finally came. The weather forecast for the 22nd wasn't great but it was still holding. It was now or never, we would be leaving the next day for our own summit push! A mix of emotions washed over me as I realized this was IT—the decision was made and the culmination of everything we had worked so intensely for was finally within our grasp. I felt a lump forming in my throat. I knew I was ready for this. Denise was ready for this. But in the back of my mind, I also knew that monsoon season was upon us and maybe the decision to wait would be a horrible mistake. But, mistake or not, we were finally going for it.

We had a team meeting to discuss our plans and make a final review of the critical days ahead. We needed to make sure we were packing all of the essential food and climbing gear, and nothing extra. Every ounce added up and carrying extra weight could compromise our speed and safety and even make the difference between reaching the summit or not. Scott had asked us all to bring our packs down for this meeting to do one last gear check. I pulled out all of the essential items he was looking to check off his list, plus one more—the Sarah Bear! The look of disapproval and bewilderment on his face said it all. I imagined him thinking; "Why on earth would Paul need to carry a stuffed Teddy bear with him for this critical part of our mission? Sure, we're headed up to a really scary part of the mountain with questionable weather, but is this guy so afraid that he needs a Teddy bear to help him sleep at night?" After explaining the significance of this bear to Scott and showing him the little plastic prosthetic leg, he was mildly receptive. "How much does that thing weigh?" he said as he picked it up to gauge the number of extra ounces involved. I actually contemplated at that moment cutting open its belly to pull out all of the stuffing to reduce the weight a bit. In addition to the symbolic importance of carrying the bear for the sake of CAF and our Everybody to Everest group, Brian Lorenz the owner of the company who makes the Sarah Bears, agreed to make a large donation to CAF if we got it to the summit and took a picture. With this in mind and despite Scott's disapproving glare, we made the decision not to desecrate the Sarah Bear and to take her along for the trip.

The alarm on my altimeter watch went off at 1:30 a.m. and with a surge of anticipation-filled adrenaline we were once again moving with a mission. The plan was to leave Base Camp at 3 a.m. to make it through the Khumbu Icefall and safely to Camp 2 before the temperature got too warm. Dawa met us at the Puja stupa to join us as we paid our final ceremonial respects before circling around the altar three times. He was burning juniper boughs as he chanted Buddhist prayers and the scent of the pine oils permeated my senses and was seared into my mind. We couldn't understand the words he was saying, but could feel the intensity and conviction in this holy lama's voice. His body language punctuated the importance of the message. He didn't chant these prayers the last two times we entered the Icefall so I couldn't help but assume these were some heavy duty blessings reserved for the severity of our summit push. I squeezed Denise's hand as Dawa completed his final blessings and without any further words exchanged, he motioned for us to go.

We filed into a line and our team was finally on our way up through the treacherous Khumbu Icefall for the very last time. Somehow Ania ended up at the front of the line which slowed the group's progress considerably. She was in a weakened state after a bout with food poisoning a few days earlier from something she ate at Base Camp. I felt queasy as well after that dinner but fortunately my strength recovered much faster than Ania's. I think we were all anxious to move faster than our current slow pace, especially after witnessing several avalanches in the past weeks come crashing down through the Icefall route where we were now climbing. We all knew time was of the essence here so Denise and

I and a few others passed Ania as she did her best to trudge along in her condition with minimal fuel in her stomach.

And then in the predawn hours it happened, exactly what we had feared. A thunderous noise erupted on the slopes above. It was an avalanche! An enormous volume of snow began roaring down the slopes towards us. We all halted in our tracks but my brain was frantically running. Within milliseconds it was processing the information from this potentially catastrophic scene, in order to instruct my body how to react. The thought of Heidi Kloos living her final moments before becoming engulfed by the crushing and suffocating weight of snow flashed through my mind as well. What an agonizingly unfortunate tragedy. I felt bad for her and her family, and her dog Menke, all over again. Luckily for us, because of the contours of the slope, the avalanche followed a path just beneath us, where we had all just been climbing a short while ago. Yet we were close enough still to be dusted with snow from the aftermath of this large and powerful force. I felt the cool spray of ice crystals against my face and realized we had been well justified earlier in our anxiety to move faster. Without saying much to one another, we turned and continued climbing up at an accelerated pace.

We made it safely to Camp 1 without further incident and took a break for some Clif Bars and water. The sun started to beat down, quickly heating our skin through our jackets, so we shed some layers before heading into the Western Cwm. The unique climate of this frozen glacier continuously astonished me. To go from being chilled to the bone to sweltering and wanting to remove all of your clothing in a single hour was the most bizarre feeling, and one that I never got used to. We arrived at Camp 2 at 21,000 feet and were pleased to see all of our gear there safe and sound.

The next day was a planned rest and recovery day at Camp 2 and we mostly relaxed in our tent, thinking about the days ahead. We were still on schedule for the weather window on the 22nd. I was anxious and a bit nervous as we packed our bags. We would be moving on to Camp 3 the next day and from there the peak would be almost within reach. I could feel the excited energy racing through me—this was it.

We left Camp 2 before 6:00 a.m. on May 20th and hiked for about an hour until we approached the base of the Lhotse Face. The wind was blowing considerably and we could see the spindrift snow whipping around way up at Camp 3. But we were in our 8,000 meter Marmot down suits and had hand warmers to keep the chill away from our fingers. We were physically and mentally ready to get the job done! Scott was just a bit ahead of us and as soon as we reached him, he told us the news. Without any discussion or debate this time, he made the decision—we were turning around. My heart sank.

•  •  •  •  •

## *Step to the Summit*
## MAKE A DECISION

The word "decide" comes from the Latin root "decidere" meaning literally, "to cut off." Our team made some difficult and meaningful decisions with respect to the weather and when to attempt the summit. When we decided to wait for the later weather window, we effectively "cut off" our chances to summit on the 17th, and when Scott decided to turn us around at the base of the Lhotse Face because of the high winds, he may have "cut off" our chances altogether of reaching the summit. Although I was distraught beyond belief at the time, I fully respected the decision. He was also "cutting off" any possibility for us to be caught in a fierce

> *"Once you make a decision, the universe conspires to make it happen."*
> *—Ralph Waldo Emerson*

windstorm at Camp 3 which would have put us at great risk. Difficult decisions like these come with the territory as a mountain guide and as a leader. Scott listened to his gut, and stood by his convictions and responsibility to keep us safe.

Big decisions in business and life require courage and faith. Too often we become paralyzed by the fear of making an incorrect decision. This is particularly true when the choices are surrounded by uncertainty and ambiguity. We are concerned with how a wrong decision may affect us or our employees and others; we are concerned with how we will be judged or even judge ourselves later. Meanwhile no decision is made, causing further anguish and potential problems. Sometimes all we need to do is take a step back, remind ourselves of our core values and goals, and simply make a decision.

# JUST BREATHE

*When faced with difficult and anxiety-elevating situations,*
*engage in deep breathing. It will deliver more oxygen to the body*
*and mind and help you produce far better results.*

## THE WEATHER WINDOW IS CLOSING

My pulse was racing. What? We're not going? How could that be possible? I saw eight years of preparation flash before my eyes. All of the training and sacrifices made to get here. And now we were turning back.

I looked up to Camp 3, and saw clusters of tents dotting the landscape and clinging precariously to the slope where the wind was violently blowing plumes of snow and ice. In my heart I knew that the correct decision had been made. But still that familiar lump grew in my throat—this quite possibly could have been our last chance to attempt the summit. Making matters worse Scott and Bill had been tracking a cyclone named Laila, which had formed over the Bay of Bengal and was heading straight towards us. We later learned that Cyclone Laila prompted 45,000 people to be evacuated in India and when it made landfall, it left 16 people dead. This was one powerful storm system and if it continued its path towards Everest it would surely bring with it heavy snowfall and have a ruinous effect on climbing conditions. It's often a race against time to beat the arrival of these cyclones, which is exactly what happened on May 25th last season. Had time already run out on us this year? I tried to stay positive as Denise and I dejectedly climbed back into our tents at Camp 2. I could almost hear the disappointed thoughts in her head, "Did we really get this far only to have it all slip through our fingers? Is it really over?" My heart sank as I saw the look on her face. She too, thought we might have reached the end of our journey.

I lay down and tried to slow my rapidly beating heart. I inhaled as deeply as I could to try to relax my body and my brain (which was not an easy task at 21,500 feet). I reasoned with myself. No matter what the outcome of this trip, we had certainly done what we came here to do. We had raised over $100,000 for the Challenged Athletes Foundation, and we had helped 23 of our friends experience an adventure of a lifetime. I thought back to standing on that large rock platform in Base Camp, watching all of those blue jackets and red caps marching into camp. My heart filled with joy again and I relaxed a little. I took another deep breath and waited.

> *"Breathe. Let go. And remind yourself that this very moment is the only one you know you have for sure."*
> *—Oprah Winfrey*

Later Scott remarked that out of all four of his previous Everest expeditions, he had never seen winds that strong. We wanted desperately to be at Camp 3 now, but it was good to be sheltered somewhat from the elements, down at Camp 2. Despite the looming approach of Cyclone Laila, we were ecstatic to hear that we would be pressing on after all. The delay would set us back only one day from our previously scheduled attempt, putting our arrival at the South Col with a shot at the summit on May 23rd …assuming the weather cooperated.

We awoke to the same wind conditions in the early morning hours, but as the day progressed they seemed to subside a bit. We felt the excitement building with every step of our heavy boots, and every crunch of our crampons into the snow. Climbing up the Lhotse Face seemed almost routine now as we negotiated the steep technical sections with even more confidence and agility in our movements. The snow conditions remained optimal as we avoided a few solid blue icy spots and dragged ourselves up to Camp 3—for the last time.

On all the mountains around the world that we have climbed, Camp 3 on Everest takes the prize for the most treacherous, irrational, and seemingly improbable place to pitch a tent. It is comprised of rock-hard snow and slippery ice, all at 24,000 feet above sea level. The angle of the slope is so severe it takes considerable effort and mental alertness to simply stand in place. The tents were carefully positioned on a tiny perch carved out of this steep incline, and a fixed line was set running right in front of them for safety. It was the most bizarre feeling to crawl to the edge of our tent, peek out and see a 2,500-foot vertical drop to the valley below. If you moved around at all, you needed to make sure to clip your carabiner onto the fixed line before stepping outside the tent. Sunbeams bounce and dance off the sheets of ice; at times I felt as if I were sitting on the ledge of a mirrored skyscraper. Over the years we heard stories of people forgetting to clip into the line when leaving their tents at night to go to the bathroom, and then slipping and falling down the entire Lhotse Face to their death. Another climber, wearing only the slick bottomed inner liner of his boots, quickly lost his footing and similarly slid all the way down, meeting the same demise. With this knowledge we were extremely cautious during our time at Camp 3. We were told it was safest to just stay in our tents and food and water would be brought to us. "Room service!" I thought to myself. We already had the best room in the house so I was happy to comply and simply enjoy the view from our penthouse suite.

*Camp 3 "On the Edge." Photo by Bill Allen*

We got settled in and Scott distributed our oxygen cylinders. From this point and higher we would be continuously using supplemental oxygen for climbing and even for sleeping. The decision to use supplemental oxygen was an easy one. First of all, very few people in the world are physiologically capable of climbing Everest without it. Second, while also reducing cognitive abilities, the diminished oxygen supplied to the body's cells at this altitude increases the chances of frostbite exponentially.

Supplemental oxygen used for climbing is a different type of system compared to one used for SCUBA diving for example. A diving tank contains compressed air similar to what we breathe every day at sea level (78% nitrogen, 21% oxygen, plus trace amounts of other gases). Through the use of a SCUBA regulator, this air is forced into your lungs, effortlessly expanding them and countering the pressure of the water compressing the chest cavity while diving. A supplemental oxygen system used for climbing at high altitudes is very different. Rather than air being pushed into your lungs, it takes the same amount of effort as it would otherwise to breathe by contracting the diaphragm, expanding the chest and filling the lungs. Another difference wearing a mask with this system is that pure oxygen is mixing with the outside air within the pocket of space formed by the mask. A special rubber valve controls the flow of outside air and the result is a slightly higher percentage of oxygen flowing into your lungs to compensate for the lack of oxygen at altitude.

The oxygen tanks we were using weighed eight pounds each and had regulators attached to manually control flow rates. During climbing, you adjust the flow from 0 to 4 liters per minute in order to raise and lower the amount of pure oxygen going into your mask. The level is determined by your altitude and largely based on the amount of effort being exerted. Camp 3 was the lowest point for which we needed supplemental oxygen, and we would just be sleeping there, so we set our flow to ½ liter per minute. One bottle holds about 720 liters of oxygen, so set at ½ liter per minute the bottle would last close to 24 hours. Higher up on the mountain, the flow is set to 2, 3, or even 4 liters per minute, so the oxygen can deplete in as little as three hours on maximum flow. Since it seeps into the mask as a constant stream, you can't use more or less like you do on a SCUBA tank. It simply runs out based on the flow rate, so we needed to be diligent and conserve our precious supply. Scott had much calculating to do to allot for all of the oxygen tanks needed for our night at Camp 3, traveling from Camp 3 to Camp 4, resting at Camp 4 and then heading to the summit and back down. Because it was unknown how long the wait at Camp 4 would be, Scott really had to do a lot of math. All in all, the Sherpas stocked 108 oxygen bottles for us at Camp 4! It was a painstaking effort over the course of the preceding weeks, and without our Sherpas' help accomplishing this task, our chances of success would have been significantly diminished.

When I first hooked up my regulator, I noticed a slight hissing noise coming from somewhere in the mechanism. These were Russian-made Poisk oxygen tanks and equipment that have been used successfully on Everest for years. Nonetheless they were still Russian-made, and having spent some time in their country, we had reason to doubt the reliability. Up at this altitude, it is imperative that all equipment functions properly, especially the oxygen system. Even a small leak could cause the tank to deplete prematurely, and I certainly did not want that to happen; so Scott swapped out my regulator for another one.

Sleeping on oxygen at elevation improves rest and recovery and also helps prevent Cheyne-Stokes respiration. This is a pattern of breathing where breaths go to their maximum depth and speed and then stop completely, sometimes for periods up to 30 seconds. This is also called "periodic breathing" which is what happens during sleep apnea. Climbers have been known to wake up from a dead sleep with a horrific sensation of panic, gasping for air feeling as though they are suffocating. I have only experienced this in mild forms, high up on other mountains, and was glad to have the slight extra boost of oxygen to sleep up here. I forgot all about the fact that our tent was set precipitously near the edge of the massive slope of the Lhotse Face, and I fell asleep dreaming of the summit.

Early the next morning (Saturday, May 22nd), we clipped onto the fixed line outside our tent and began climbing to Camp 4. We looked up and noticed that approximately 40 other climbers were already on the fixed line ahead of us! We knew this was foreshadowing of what might lie ahead of us on summit day. In addition, even more climbers piled onto the line above us because there was a group of tents slightly higher up than our Camp 3 location. Our pace slowed to that of the slowest person among all of those ahead. It was like being in a long line for an amusement park ride. Although at this altitude, on this mountain, it was not very amusing.

There are a few challenging obstacles between Camp 3 and Camp 4. The first is the Yellow Band followed by the Geneva Spur. The Yellow Band is an extremely tricky section due to the fact that it is made up of hard and smooth limestone and shale rock slanted at a steep angle. The steel pointed tips of our crampons had no place to dig in or grip. Deep scratch marks on the stone left by other climbers were telltale signs indicating where not to step. We carefully placed our crampons on the rock and held our breath hoping not to hear a sound similar to nails digging into a chalkboard. One careful step at a time we made it up and over the Yellow Band.

*Approaching the Geneva Spur – 25,500 feet*

The next obstacle was the Geneva Spur, a meandering trail of rock and snow leading to a steep ridge. Climbing up and over this sheer incline requires strength and endurance; thankfully we seemed to have both in ample supply. After stepping up and over the crest of the Geneva Spur we were rewarded with a stunning view of the summit of Everest, dominating the skyline above. From there it was no more than 20 minutes along a relatively easy path to Camp 4. Six hours after leaving Camp 3, we had reached the South Col. I was running through a mental list: Lhotse Face—check. Camp 3—check. Yellow Band—check. Geneva Spur—check. Camp 4—check. It was now time to settle into our tent to rest and prepare for the biggest test of our lives.

Camp 4 at 26,000 feet is nothing more than a desolate and barren wasteland. We were happy to be there yet simultaneously intimidated to be in this graveyard-like place where many climbers have perished. We were the first of our climbing team to arrive and I took stock of our surroundings. Right next to where our amazing Sherpas had set up our tents for us, I noticed the remains of another tent lying flat on the snow and rock, obliterated to shreds by the wind. Aluminum tent poles protruded and crisscrossed through the ripped nylon, almost like the exposed bones of an animal carcass deteriorating in the harsh elements. I shuddered to think of what could have possibly happened to the climbers who previously occupied that tent. I thought of all those who had been here before me—those who had reached the pinnacle of their journeys, those who had fallen just short, and those who had lost their lives here.

I looked across the vast expanse of the Col and couldn't help but think again of the 1996 disaster recounted by Krakauer in "Into Thin Air." It was here at the South Col where Beck Weathers, Charlotte Fox, Sandy Pittman, Tim Madson, Yasuko Namba, and guides Mike Groom and Neil Beidleman all fought for their lives. They were desperately searching for their tents in the dark during a terrible whiteout and fierce storm. They huddled together in the biting cold for hours here, where we were now, and not all of them survived. In total during the '96 season on Everest, there were 98 people who reached the summit and 15 deaths. Applying that startling statistic of 15% to the seven members of our own team equates to one death amongst us. I hoped and prayed nothing bad would happen to any of us nor to any climbers from other teams who were also assembling here.

Denise and I climbed into our tent and changed our oxygen bottles. We organized our gear, filled our water bottles and tried to get as many calories into ourselves as possible. We hoped to be properly fueled for an enormous physical ordeal that was expected to begin shortly after nightfall. We knew however, from talking with Dr. Hackett previously, that our bodies would only be able to assimilate a small portion of the protein and carbohydrates we were ingesting.

*Camp 4 – South Col – 26,000 feet. Photo by Scott Woolums*

Here at the South Col we were now in the "Death Zone." This region at 26,000 feet and above gained its name not because of the number of deaths that have occurred here, but because of what happens to your body physiologically at this altitude. There is simply not enough oxygen in the air for the human body to survive, even well acclimatized bodies like ours, so it essentially begins shutting down. Processes like digestion of food require oxygen, and when it is in limited supply, the body must ration the available oxygen for more vital functions (such as for operating the heart, lungs, and brain). As a result we wouldn't get as much of the value of the food we were eating, instead that energy would come from the glycogen already stored in our muscles. Up here, our bodies were in essence feeding off of themselves. We couldn't afford to stay here too long.

Denise and I tried to sleep, knowing this would be our last chance to rest before being given the green light in a few hours to leave for the summit. The wind was strong and had really picked up, howling through camp and beating against the sides of our tent. We looked

139

at each other cautiously and held our breath when Bill came to us to give an update on the weather. Yelling over the thunderous sound of the nylon tents flapping he said, "It doesn't look good for us to go up tonight, it's just too windy."

Not again, I thought. Not another day lost because of the weather? ...I don't want to wait around in this place...we're in the Death Zone here!

• • • • •

— *Step to the Summit* —
## JUST BREATHE

> *"He lives most life whoever breathes most air."*
> *—Elizabeth Barrett Browning*

When the wind is taken out of your sails, and you let out a big sigh of disappointment in the boardroom or in life, it's time to just breathe. Our bodies have the ability to function for days without food, water, and sleep, but can survive only moments without air. Yet surprisingly enough, breathing properly is not something many people know how to do. Breathing is not only a physiological function; it is psychological as well. Breathing properly allows you to oxygenate your cells to promote optimal brain function. Even at sea level, stress and anxiety cause us to breathe in a more shallow, stunted manner, starving our body and mind of the vital oxygen it needs. In some respects it is akin to putting yourself into the Death Zone. This type of shallow breathing is, of course, the exact opposite of what you need to do when dealing with stressful circumstances.

In the practice of yoga, your "prana" is the energy you extract from the air. The more prana you have in your body, the more alive you are as a whole. So why not then maximize the amount of air we take into our lungs? Stop for a moment and take a deep breath. Could you have taken more air into your lungs? Try again, this time pushing out your belly first filling up the bottom portion of your lungs. Then during the same inhale, push your shoulders back to expand your chest, and take in even more air, filling up the top portion of your lungs next. Hold your breath for a brief count, and slowly exhale pushing out all of that used air. Repeat this routine several times. Not only will you feel more relaxed, you will also be giving your body and brain a significant advantage over the vast majority of people, perhaps even your competitors in business, who never learned how to breathe properly! Imagine, you can actually be healthier and smarter (and improve your chances of reaching the top) if you Just Breathe.

# NEVER GIVE UP

*When the slope is steep and your progress seems slow,*
*keep moving towards your goal. If you keep taking steps forward*
*and never give up, you will eventually reach your summit.*

## GRIPPING THE EDGE OF THE EARTH

After taking a deep breath and accepting the unfortunate news about the weather, we decided to relax and close our eyes for a bit. We awoke from our nap to a commotion outside our tent. Voices were raised, there was yelling back and forth between the nylon walls. We couldn't make out exactly what they were saying, but then we heard, "We're leaving for the summit in 15 minutes!" Denise and I looked at each other, our eyes wide with excitement behind our oxygen masks and said, "We're doing this!" We scrambled to get all of our gear together as quickly as possible and mentally checked off critical items on our list one by one. I had a flashback to our guest bedroom at home, all of our gear and supplies lined up ready to be packed for the adventure of a lifetime. We filled our water bottles, ripped open our hand and foot warmers, and packed the camera and extra snacks. We put on our boots and climbing harnesses, and attached our headlamps to our helmets. Then we put on our crampons, changed to fresh oxygen cylinders and finally turned our backs on the shelter of our tents and headed out of Camp 4. Hopefully the next time we would see this place would be after a successful summit.

It was 9 p.m. on May 22nd. Stars sparkled brightly in the sky and the partial moon reflected a gleaming light off the snow, revealing the mammoth peak we were about to tackle. We felt relieved and excited that we were finally able to get this last and most significant part of our journey started. After all the weeks of acclimatization hikes, the gear preparation, the agonizing waiting for acceptable weather, concerns about staying healthy for the duration of the expedition and the non-stop "what if" jitters, we finally reached the moment of truth. The game was on! All there was to do now was simply CLIMB.

The glow of headlamp after headlamp illuminated the path ahead of us. It was a beautiful sight but a concern at the same time. We counted more than three dozen people already winding their way up the steep climbing route above. We knew it would be a busy night with so many other climbers waiting for the same break in the weather as we were. It was just surprising that so many other teams were getting such an early start as this. As we experienced earlier in the morning climbing up from Camp 3 to Camp 4, we could only move as fast as the slowest person in the long line ahead of us. I wished we could be further ahead in that line, but at this point I was simply relieved to be going at all and heading toward our goal. There was such excitement in the air; several of our Sherpas had never been to the summit so they were just as eager as we were to be finally making the climb to the top. All in total, there were 18 in our group for this final leg: 5 climbers, 2 guides and 11 Sherpas. This was an unusually large number of Sherpas, most teams are considered well supported if there is a one-to-one Sherpa to climber ratio. However, Dawa and Scott wanted to reward some of the Sherpas who had worked hard for them on previous Everest expeditions but weren't able to go to the top. Once Sherpas have an Everest summit to their credit, their socioeconomic status skyrockets and they are virtually guaranteed to be hired on subsequent expeditions. We were on our way with a solid crew. One Sherpa stayed back at Camp 4 in case of an emergency. I desperately hoped there wouldn't be one.

The pace began to slow considerably as we headed into steeper terrain, and after about 30 minutes the long line ahead of us began to back up. There were at least another 40 people behind us now, so we were literally smack dab in the middle of a bona fide traffic jam. Scott would later say that this was the most crowded he had ever seen the mountain. Rocks zoomed past our faces, as they were knocked loose from climbers above. I got pelted in the thigh by a large tumbling object and was extremely grateful that it turned out to be a compacted clump of snow. Had it been a rock that hit me with the same velocity, my climb would likely have been over.

There were a number of small rock ledges over which the fixed rope had to clear, and consequently this made it extremely difficult for some people to get their ascenders and themselves up and over the obstacle. When this occurred it brought the entire lineup to a dead stop, sometimes for as long as ten to fifteen minutes. This frustrating stopping and starting again became the routine for much of the night.

Our concerns about the slow rate of progress were twofold. First, we had a limited supply of oxygen, and at the current pace we could very well run out, forcing us to turn around before reaching the summit. Our second concern was about getting cold while waiting for these delays ahead of us. As long as we were moving, our blood was flowing and we were generating body heat. I remembered Valerie whom we met at Base Camp and her advice to us to keep moving at all costs on summit day. She paid the price for failing to do so and had to have her toes amputated.

> *"When you come to the end of your rope, tie a knot and hang on."*
> **—Franklin D. Roosevelt**

Frostbite is the one thing I desperately wanted to avoid. Extreme sub-zero temperatures such as what we were experiencing cause your body to go into preservation mode, and your blood vessels automatically constrict. When this happens, the body's priority is to protect the core, especially the heart and brain, so the areas furthest from it (like your fingers and toes) may be sacrificed for survival. The blood vessels become damaged by the cold, so blood flow to the extremities is halted and tissue can die.

I noticed that even with hand warmers in both gloves, my left hand seemed to be getting cold from all of this waiting around. Then my thoughts turned to my right hand, my injured hand that didn't have nearly the same nerve sensations as my left. I couldn't help but think back to the Carstenz Pyramid climb and how I wasn't even aware that I had cut my right arm as severely as I had. Although it didn't feel cold I started to wonder if my right hand was at risk as well.

We continued to make our way slowly up the mountain throughout the dark and cold night. It was probably after 1:00 a.m. when we passed the area where Scott Fisher's body has remained since he took his last breath in 1996. And then Denise told me she was having a problem. She noticed an issue with the rubber exhale valve of her oxygen mask. She thought it was coming loose and asked me to help. Denise was climbing in front of me so she turned around so I could see what was going on. I was astonished to see that the entire valve had completely fallen off! That piece is a critical component of the mask as it is meant to inhibit non-oxygenated air from freely flowing into the mask. This meant she had been climbing without the proper amount of oxygen to her lungs. We had no idea how much oxygen she had been getting all this time; and how much she hadn't been getting. We had no means to fix the mask. By now we were even further into the Death Zone. I thought back to our previous talks about what we would do if one of us couldn't continue and needed to turn back. Had that moment arrived? I thought about the release forms we had signed before our trip, especially the Body Disposal & Repatriation Form. We had definitely reached the part of the mountain where they don't bring you back down. I wasn't going to take that risk with either one of us. I thought it might be time to turn back.

Bill was climbing behind us and I asked him whether he was carrying a spare oxygen mask. He was not but told us that one of the Sherpas should have one. There was some back and forth chatter in Nepali about it as we continued to climb, but no oxygen mask was produced.

We forged ahead nonetheless, making our way up towards the Balcony at 27,500 feet, which is roughly the halfway point between Camp 4 and the summit. This was our planned spot to regroup and change oxygen cylinders. As we climbed on I asked again about the mask and it was relayed back to us by one of the Sherpas that we would have to wait until we got to the Balcony. Every moment that went by concerned me that Denise might be in danger because she wasn't getting enough oxygen. She seemed to be communicating in a lucid manner and her pace didn't slow down. I would have expected more lethargic movement from somebody climbing without any oxygen at all. So either she was managing to get at least some minor oxygen flow from the malfunctioning mask, or she was extremely fit and aerobically strong from all the training we had done. Perhaps it was a combination of the two. Nevertheless we kept climbing and hoping every five minutes or so that the Balcony would be just up ahead. This went on for over an hour. At last we reached our destination, the spot where we would, with any luck, be able to find our salvation for the continuation of the climb—a spare oxygen mask.

Reaching the Balcony was a relief but also a bit chaotic. The Balcony is an unusually rare piece of flat real estate within a landscape otherwise dominated by steep slopes. Different groups of climbers were crammed together shoulder-to-shoulder on this platform that was no bigger than a small motel room. Our down climbing suits all looked similar and with oxygen masks and goggles covering faces it was difficult to locate the other members of our team. Luckily, we found Dawang Chhu and he located a spare oxygen mask for Denise. We swapped it out along with our tanks. As we left the Balcony I still worried about the possible damage that Denise had already suffered. She had been without proper oxygen for at least an hour. But she was determined to continue on and had already clipped back into the line and started climbing again. I silently said a prayer for her safety and jumped back into line behind her.

I was looking forward to sunrise. This had been the coldest part of the night and since we were moving so slowly, it was difficult to keep our bodies warm. After the Balcony, there were several technical rock sections to climb. It was slowing people down considerably. The line halted again to a dead stop. I likened it to sitting in traffic on the busiest freeways in Los Angeles. However, two words we never heard were, "Hurry up!" I have noticed throughout my eight years traveling the world climbing the Seven Summits, that mountaineers are generally quite respectful of one another. Even in a situational "parking lot" type traffic jam such as this one, there was no road rage to be had. Maybe we were all thinking it, but everyone kept their virtual "horn honking" to themselves. We simply needed to be patient. Becoming frustrated with the climbers ahead was not going to solve our problem. Still, hours and hours had passed and I wondered if there were enough oxygen tanks for us and for all of these other people on the mountain. Just then a yellow glow began to emanate from the horizon over China and Tibet. It was the most spectacularly breathtaking and welcomed sunrise I have ever witnessed. It was still bitterly cold when the bright rays of the sun finally hit us. Although the temperature rose only slightly, our spirits soared when we were able to see the magnificent Himalayan peaks below us from this heavenly vantage point.

*Rush hour traffic above The Balcony – 27,900 feet*

We hoisted ourselves up and over the last of the rock ledges and then Scott suggested we take a break so the rest of the team members could catch up. We pulled our headlamps off of our helmets and I figured it was a good opportunity to take a drink. I reached into the inner pocket of my down suit where I kept my Platypus bottle so it wouldn't freeze. I took a drink and accidentally squeezed the bottle the wrong way, squirting the liquid onto my left glove. I almost didn't realize at the time that I had gotten my glove wet, because the water had frozen instantly so there was not even a wet sheen to it. Unbeknownst to me, my glove had lost some of its insulating properties as a result. As we continued on, I noticed that my hand had grown progressively colder, yet I still hadn't connected it to the spill. I tried retracting my fingers within the glove, pulling them back from the individual finger separations in order to make a fist and keep them warmer. This was marginally helpful but cost me the ability to grip or otherwise use my fingers. I desperately needed my left hand to clench and operate the release lever on my ascender; or it would be impossible to go any farther. Because of my BPI my right hand is simply not strong enough to operate an ascender, even in the best of circumstances. The bottom line - I needed my left hand. I slid my fingers back into the cold and frozen finger slots of my glove so I could continue climbing. I knew I couldn't go on much longer like this or I would be inviting serious frostbite for sure. My thoughts flashed back to Ochiai again, the Japanese climber we met in Antarctica, who lost all ten fingers to frostbite, right here on Everest. I was not about to lose any fingers, especially on my left hand which I rely on for everything. It's not in my nature to give up, but turning around was looking to be the only prudent option now. I needed a solution, and I needed it fast.

If there was ever a time for me to draw upon my creativity, as I did to create the Claw in order to climb Carstensz Pyramid, that time was right now. I thought back to my years as a swimmer and how we would warm up our shoulders before a workout or swim meet. I began to swing my entire arm around and around in a circular motion, trying to stimulate blood flow to my fingers through centrifugal force. Then a searing pain shot through my hand. It felt like a thousand knives were stuck under my skin, traveling to each of my fingers, their sharp points hitting every nerve along the way. As painful as this felt, I was so ecstatic I wanted to cry. It was working! If I could feel the pain it was a good sign as I knew numbness always precedes frostbite. I was in the clear; nothing was going to stop me from reaching the summit now. Or so I thought.

We had been climbing for about 11 hours. We hadn't accounted for so many climbers and such a slow pace. It was about 8:00 a.m. and we were at 28,500 feet, higher than the summit of K2, the earth's second highest peak. It had taken us much longer than Scott had hoped to get to our current location. At that point I just about lost my oxygen-deprived mind when he said, "I don't know if we're going to have time to go all the way to the top."

What? Are you kidding me? We've come this far and we're going to turn around now? His comment didn't seem to make any sense. We were doing great, feeling strong, and the weather seemed to be holding up, other than some clouds building on the Tibetan side of the mountain. I thought to myself, we didn't pay all of this money, spend years preparing and take two months away from work to climb *almost* all the way to the top of Everest. I guess he was just thinking aloud again because we kept going and eventually reached our next oxygen cache at the South Summit. It was here at 28,700 feet where Scott, Denise, and I stopped again to change our oxygen cylinders and wait for the rest of our team.

Tarke Sherpa was with us and he was on the radio talking to the other Sherpas down below and also talking to Scott. I couldn't make out exactly what they were saying over the noise of the wind, which had picked up considerably. I was motioning for Tarke to hand over the cylinders to us so we could change them and continue on, but he seemed to be stalling for some reason. I took the opportunity to retrieve my summit mitts from my pack hoping these would keep my hands warmer. Then Scott expressed even more concern about continuing on, but didn't make any definitive statements about turning back. Tarke finally handed over the oxygen cylinders for us and helped us change them out. By now Ania, Cindy, and several other Sherpas had caught up to us here, just beyond the South Summit, and they continued on.

With fresh oxygen cylinders now, Denise and I clipped back onto the fixed rope to continue going up. I didn't even look at Scott, fearing what he might say about turning around. Instead we just quickly filed in behind Karma Sherpa, one of the youngest and strongest Sherpas on our team. As I set off I heard Scott say, "I think this is a bad idea." I knew in the back of my mind that he had made the right calls about turning around before, but this time I just couldn't give in. He didn't tell us to stop, so we just kept going with an unsettled feeling that he might know something that we didn't.

With this concern rattling around in the back of our minds, our next challenge was crossing the Cornice Traverse. This is an unusually narrow ridgeline of wind-swept snow with scarcely enough room to place both boots side by side. This ridge also forms the border between China and Nepal. If you were to slip unroped to the left, you would fall 8,000 vertical feet down the Southwest Face into Nepal. Slipping to the right meant a fall of 10,000 vertical feet down the Kangshung Face into China. The wind continued to blow from the right, testing our balance and pushing us to the Nepal side of the ridgeline; probably a better alternative considering we didn't have tourist visas for China!

Once again my left hand and particularly my thumb were both getting cold. I was also having trouble operating the release mechanism on my ascender with the mitt on, so I stopped again and one of the Sherpas helped me get my frozen glove back out of my pack. I swapped it with the mitt and was again able to operate the ascender. I prayed that my hand would warm back up.

Immediately after the Cornice Traverse, the Hillary Step is the last technical section before the summit. I had read all about the Hillary Step and the strength needed to hoist your entire body up and over this roughly 40 foot high rock and snow covered wall. For years I thought this spot right here would be an insurmountable obstacle for me to ever climb Mt. Everest. I had the Claw device ready in my pack for my right hand but was reluctant to stop again to pull it out. I decided I would try my best and use all of the strength I could muster with my left hand. I knew it would be a strain and require everything I had, especially considering the fact we had been climbing for almost 12 hours straight at this point.

I did however have an additional reserve of power inside my pack. It was a 12" x 16" piece of thin yellow nylon bearing the CAF logo. It also contained the names of 80 of our closest friends who each contributed $290 or more to CAF on our behalf. We were climbing the mountain for them as well, and I could actually feel their energy and incredible support for us and for such a worthy cause as CAF. Tapping into this emotional reservoir I mustered all of the brute force I could summon from my left arm, and with one more enormous pull, I was on top of the Hillary Step! Each and every one of these friends, including challenged athletes like "One-Arm Willie" Stewart, Scout Bassett, Sarah Reinertsen, John Siciliano and so many others are the ones who pulled me up and over this last hurdle to reach the goal.

My pulse quickened. This was it! I could actually see it in front of me. There was nothing left to do but climb the last few steps to the very top. It had been 12 hours since we left Camp 4 at the South Col. It had been seven weeks to the day since we had said goodbye to our loved ones on Easter Sunday. Throughout all of the challenges and overwhelming hurdles we had faced, we never gave up. I handed my video camera to Bill and heard him narrating like a news reporter as we took our final steps, "Here come Paul and Denise Fejtek, just feet from the summit of Mt. Everest, May 23rd, about 9:30 in the morning..." Denise pulled her mask off and screamed, "We made it! Wooohoo!" I took my mask off and kissed my wife. I could hear Bill continuing to talk to the camera, "The top of the world..."

That's when it hit me. We were on the top of the world. We had climbed all the way up to 29,029 feet, the cruising altitude of a jetliner. The view was beyond stunning and I didn't have to peer out of a tiny airplane window to see it. It was right there in front of my eyes. Several of the world's highest peaks were within view and here they stood in their majestic glory, beneath us, shrouded by billowing clouds. I thought of my childhood and my mother cheering me on through swim meets, water skiing, and judo practice. I thought of my marriage and having an incredible partner like Denise by my side for almost every milestone and success of my adult life. I thought of all the amazing people in my life: my family, my friends, our Everybody to Everest group, our guides and Sherpas, and the remarkable people at CAF who inspired me to embark on this incredible eight-year adventure. I took the video camera and did a 360-degree pan from the summit. "We're on top of the world," I said to the camera. "Number seven of the Seven Summits!" Denise looked at me and grinned. I think at that moment it hit her too.

We had done it.

*On top of the world – Mt. Everest – May 23, 2010*

*Step to the Summit*
## NEVER GIVE UP

> *"Many of life's failures are people who did not realize how close they were to success when they gave up."*
> *—Thomas Edison*

Standing atop the absolute highest point on earth, and enduring all it took to get there, gave me a better perspective of the world. I thought about all of the things I had achieved in my life because I never gave up. I thought about all of the steps I had taken to reach the summit:

| | |
|---|---|
| Dream Big and Step Up | Have a Little Faith |
| Live Courageously | Move Fast |
| Discover Your Creativity | Take a Step Back |
| Be Determined & Disciplined | Maintain a Sharp Focus |
| Lead and They Will Follow | Build Quality Relationships |
| Be Prepared | Make a Decision |
| Don't Worry Be Happy | Just Breathe |

I realized that repeating some of the steps over and over again is the ultimate secret to getting to the top. Things may not always work out for us in business and in life, but when progress is slow on the way to the summit, and the obstacles seem insurmountable, above all else—Never Give Up! As the Japanese proverb goes, "Fall down seven times, get up eight times."

And remember when you help others along the route on this long climb we call life, you will end up helping yourself as well. Do not hesitate for a moment to take action and make a difference right now, and reach for *your* S.U.M.M.I.T.! Because you can be assured that **S**uccess **U**ltimately **M**eans **M**aking an **I**mpact **T**oday!

# EPILOGUE

Although we did in fact reach the summit and shared a congratulatory kiss on top of the world, this was really no place to celebrate. After taking our requisite videos and photos, including one with the Sarah Bear and the CAF summit banner, we knew it was time to head back down. We had spent about 45 minutes on the top, longer than on any of the other Seven Summits. The enormity of what we had done was overwhelming, but the reality that we were at the halfway point quickly set in. The storm had been rolling in slowly and the buildup of clouds on the Tibetan side of the mountain was looking ominous.

*"Go confidently in the direction of your dreams. Live the life you have imagined."*
—*Henry David Thoreau*

We focused ourselves on the descent and started heading down from the summit of Mt. Everest without even looking back. In retrospect I would have enjoyed one final glance at this place we had worked so hard to reach, knowing it was unlikely we would ever see it again in our lifetimes. We carefully made our way down the Hillary Step, across the Cornice Traverse and back down the ridgeline towards the Balcony and eventually the South Col. All in total our trip to the summit and back down to Camp 4 was 18½ hours! The storm was definitely here, snow was accumulating and we were relieved to crawl back into our tent and be sheltered from the elements. We weren't in the clear yet; it was 3:30 in the afternoon and we had one more night to spend in the Death Zone.

The next morning we pushed back the snow that was threatening to cave in the walls of our tent, and anxiously packed up to get the heck out of this place. As the snow continued to fall, we went back over the Geneva Spur, through the Yellow Band, and down the Lhotse Face. We finally reached Camp 2 where we assessed the condition of our battered and depleted bodies and spent another night. The following morning we left Camp 2 with all of our belongings plus a few empty oxygen cylinders to lighten the load for our Sherpas, and we finally took our last trip through the dangerous Khumbu Icefall. We were exhausted and exhilarated. Near the bottom of the Icefall we were greeted by Dawa and the rest of the Sherpas who had remained in Base Camp while we were up high on the mountain. They were anxiously awaiting our arrival to congratulate us on our success. I gave Dawa a big hug and expressed my gratitude. I told him that those special prayers he had said for us at the Puja altar before we left for our summit bid seven days ago, had really worked. When we got back in to Base Camp, we unzipped our tent and fell face first onto our sleeping bags and took a long nap.

We were awakened by a call from Surki that dinner was ready. Oh, did we miss Surki during the many days above 21,000 feet! We enjoyed the most delicious and satisfying meal of the entire expedition that night. The celebration was particularly sweet because every single member of our team: Ania, Vivian, Cindy, Scott, and Bill all made it to the summit as well. We were the only major expedition team on Everest (other than a few one and two-man teams) to have a 100% summit success rate! After dinner we danced to traditional Sherpa music and drank and enjoyed our last moments with our wonderful new Sherpa friends who had become like family.

And just like that, it was over.

Coming home after nearly two months in the Himalayas was a bit of an adjustment. I remember going back to work Monday morning and sitting down at my desk. It was a familiar place of course, but at the same time it was strangely foreign. My desk was clean and uncluttered and I ran my fingers (all ten of them) across the wood grain surface. I thought back to how cold my fingers had been up on the Hillary Step at

28,750 feet. And then the phone rang. It was such an unfamiliar sound and the noise startled me. I actually jumped and remember my heart started racing. I was quickly pulled back to reality. It was time to take back the reins on my big medical device acquisition.

Shortly after our return, we threw a big party that we dubbed, "Everfest 2010." All of our friends and family, and our amazing Everybody to Everest team came to celebrate and donate some more funds to CAF. NBC News aired a follow-up segment and our Seven Summits story was also featured on the #1 rated morning show in America, The Today Show. Sunday Show co-anchor and field correspondent Jenna Wolfe, along with producer Lindsay Grubb, both flew out from New York prior to our trip to spend a day training with us in California. They incorporated some of the video we shot from the summit and created a truly inspiring segment for their audience of millions. Most of all we were thrilled with the exposure for CAF and touched by the many responses from complete strangers.

I was overjoyed that after more than a year of hard work and the generosity of so many, our Everybody to Everest fundraising efforts had generated over $114,000 for CAF. Later that fall I was honored with CAF's Most Inspirational Athlete of the Year award and was humbled to be in such amazing company as those challenged athletes who had inspired me to push so hard and overcome obstacles in the first place. I was also awarded an entry to compete in the Ironman Triathlon World Championship in Hawaii—the Super Bowl in the sport of triathlon. Not long after my return from Everest, the training began again.

On May 23, 2011, exactly one year to the day that Denise and I reached the summit, I finally closed that big medical device deal! I had been working on the transaction for over two years. After its devastating failure just prior to leaving for Everest, it actually fell apart two more times with two different buyers. I definitely maintained a "Never Give Up" attitude and after the challenging climb to the closing table was finally complete, the press release touted: "Hunter Wise Securities announced today that its client, leading privately-held spinal implant device maker SeaSpine, Inc., has been acquired by Integra LifeSciences Holdings Corporation (NASDAQ: IART) for $89 million in cash. " I firmly believe this is just one example validating the importance of following the Steps to the Summit in business. Methodically practicing and adopting the Steps as habit, will lead you to the pinnacle of success pursuing your own summits in business and life!

*After the tremendous success of the Everybody to Everest initiative, Paul and Denise Fejtek decided to do it all over again. They have organized a similar group charity endeavor called CAFrica to climb Mt. Kilimanjaro in 2012 with a large group of friends. In between negotiating M&A deals and Paul & Denise's professional speaking engagements, the dynamic couple is also planning to lead outdoor adventure-based management retreats for corporate leadership development.*

If you enjoyed this story, gained insights of value and feel others might benefit as well, please help us by purchasing additional copies of *Steps to the Summit* at: **http://StepsToTheSummit.com**. Give copies to your friends, family, business associates, clients, and employees so they can make an Impact Today. Make recommendations and share this link on Facebook, LinkedIn, Twitter and other social media sites. By doing this and by purchasing additional copies, you will also be making an impact in the lives of deserving challenged athletes. One hundred percent of profits from the sale of this book go to CAF to help kids, American soldiers wounded in Iraq and Afghanistan, and others with disabilities or missing limbs. For more information also visit **www.challengedathletes.org**.

# REFLECTIONS FROM
# THE EVERYBODY TO
# EVEREST TEAM

As we Take a Step Back (Step #10) to appreciate where we have been, it's quite meaningful to listen to the perspectives of those who have shared the path on the journey. An extraordinary group of 23 individuals played an integral role in our *Steps to the Summit*, and I would like to introduce each of them to you. These great friends and family are all important to us but they are listed here by rank order according to the amount of funds raised for CAF. We asked each of them to reflect upon the trip and how the entire experience impacted their lives. Many of the responses are personally revealing and also profound:

Karen Robinson was the top fundraiser of the group and I got to know her through financial circles many years ago. She was a banker who had previously provided acquisition financing for me on some of my deals. Karen's trip to Base Camp was a huge sacrifice as she left at home a teenage daughter and a husband who was recovering from treatment of a brain tumor.

*"The trek and, more importantly, the reason for it (to raise money to support CAF), gave me a positive focus at a difficult time in my life. The physical fatigue of hiking all day quieted my mind and allowed me to take in all the surrounding beauty; it gave me a feeling of peace that was elusive on the home front. Also, the simple and contented life of the people in the Khumbu is*

*a great example of what is a "need" versus a "want." The Buddhist attributes of patience and acceptance are worthy of emulation. This, more than anything, has helped me to live more in the moment in my life back home with all of it's 'noise', disruptions, and struggles."*     —Karen Robinson

My sister Tina Pauley is a business development consultant for a fitness company and she was one of the first to express interest in going to Base Camp. Tina was also the one who introduced us to CAF back in 1998 and her dedication and fundraising efforts for the foundation were truly an inspiration. The hike up to Base Camp includes crossing many suspension bridges strung high over rushing streams, which forced Tina to overcome a huge fear —her fear of heights. She also made some life-changing decisions along the way.

*"After considerable thought and introspection while on the trip, I came home and within seven days I ended a relationship that just wasn't working. Less than a month later I met a wonderful, caring, athletic individual whom I love dearly and hope to spend the rest of my life with!"*

—Tina Pauley

My niece Stacie Fejtek is a marine ecologist who has been to many remote locations around the world conducting underwater research. She has a zest for life that is infectious.

*"Everybody to Everest was as much of an emotional journey as a physical journey for me. After my return I found out my mother had passed the day we made it to base camp. I found myself trying to figure out what to do with my life and frankly I felt a little lost as I think many people do after the loss of a parent."*     —Stacie Fejtek

With the inspiration of her time on Everest, Stacie dove back into her marine biology roots and took a six-month sabbatical with a research group in Santa Cruz. Months later, she was married with many of her new Everybody to Everest friends in attendance at the wedding ceremony.

Greg Hancock is a classmate of mine from college. He is an advertising executive for a large national publication. He left his wife and two kids at home to join the group for the three-week trek.

*"I have spent my life focused on my future—constantly thinking about my career path, how to make more money to support my family and how to invest that money for financial security. As I hiked to Base Camp, I found myself doing something very similar. I spent hours hiking, looking at the mountain ahead, focused on the challenge of how far we had to go – how many more days, how many more hours, how many more miles, how many more steps? At one point along our journey, standing on the edge of a path, looking through the valley behind me, I could see the path we'd been hiking. I could see where we started and just how far we had come... and I was proud. It was at that moment I realized I needed to do that in my life as well. Looking forward is important, but it's also critical to stop and realize how far I've come. Take time to step back, quit stressing about the future and celebrate the accomplishments, celebrate the successes, celebrate the life I've lived, not just the life I want to live."* —Greg Hancock

Colin Campbell is a younger fraternity brother of mine. Prior to the trip he was a financial advisor and has an incredible perspective on life for someone his age.

*"The experiences of working with CAF athletes, being passionate about a cause, and delving into another culture as deeply as we did were absolutely transformative. It brought into stark relief what is really important; that happiness is the pursuit of life and is too often obscured by the noise and fury of everyday life. The perspective that I returned home with led me to reevaluate the track that I was on, professionally and personally. Happiness and success are not mutually exclusive, and the fear of failure often is a person's biggest obstacle. There are people that overcome that obstacle, like the CAF athletes, everyday. Failure and fear can be embraced and used as a motivating factor to create a positive change, either in your life or in the world. The experience I had in Nepal helped me to realize that I have a limited time to make the significant impact I want to make."* —Colin Campbell

Upon his return from Nepal, Colin voluntarily left his prior career and made the leap to start his own company. He also returned to school to get his MBA, focusing on Social Enterprise and Impact Investment.

Rod Evans is a software engineer from Palo Alto. Originally from the UK, Rod has a great passion for exploring the outdoors and a genuine interest in learning about others.

*"The trek to Everest provided a window into a different world. From the awe and inspiration of the Himalayas and those who climb their peaks, to the simplicity of local life, and chaotic congestion of Kathmandu. I came back from this trip with a new appreciation for how different life can be for some, and perhaps how I should in some ways start living my own life in a different and more powerful and meaningful way."* —Rod Evans

Mike McCarthy is an entrepreneur and former colleague of mine in investment banking.

*"For me, Everybody to Everest represented an opportunity to fulfill a longtime goal of seeing Mt. Everest and the Himalayas. Although not a group traveler normally, taking this trip to Base Camp with the big Everybody to Everest group exceeded all my expectations and became the trip of a lifetime. The most important lesson I learned is to "enjoy the journey." Taking that adjustment to my mindset home has had a profound positive influence on how I now look at life, relationships and giving back."* —Mike McCarthy

Upon his return from Nepal, Mike initiated a successful fundraising campaign of his own and committed to a yearly effort of contribution to worthy causes. Also, in a strange twist of fate he met a very good childhood friend of mine at our Everest welcome home party, and now the two are engaged to be married.

Shawn Sedlacek owns an event marketing company. He is my fraternity brother and roommate from college. He was the best man at our wedding and actually climbed three of the Seven Summits with us.

*"The trip to Everest Base Camp was a turning point in my life. It was on that mountain that I realized the next decisions I made would change my life forever."* —Shawn Sedlacek

Sara Neilson is the Managing Director of a country club. She and Shawn had been dating for four years, and after the bonding experience of such an enormous journey as a couple and some time for tranquil reflection on the trip, Shawn decided to propose after they returned home, and they were married soon after.

*"I never dreamed of climbing a mountain. It was a big stretch for me. It was proof positive how a team can make the individual go beyond one's limit. And now I get to share the memories of this amazing experience with Shawn for the rest of our lives."* —Sara Neilson

Bryce Cripe is a financial analyst for a global investment management firm and fellow alumni from my university.

*"I had always had an adventurous spirit, but was yearning for a defining 'grand adventure'. The Everybody to Everest trek gave me that opportunity-- and with the added benefit of the higher purpose of raising funds for Challenged Athletes. I had never travelled outside North America and made the decision that I would dive head first into international travel by going to the foot of Everest. The adventure did not disappoint. The things we saw, experiences we shared and the people we met made a profound impression. I returned with a new sense of purpose and priority. After having a 'life experience' it was time to start 'living life'. Instead of continuing to allow my professional life to lead me, I resolved to focus more on enhancing other aspects of life—personal experiences, interests, friendships and relationships. It continues to be a work in progress, but whenever I feel the balance swing away from me, I think back to my Everybody to Everest experiences to bring things back into perspective."* —Bryce Cripe

Camille Attell is a learning and development manager for a global investment management firm (sound familiar?). Bryce invited her along on the trip and during the experience a relationship developed beyond that of a friendly office acquaintance.

*"I feel very lucky to have been a member of The Everybody to Everest team and consider the Himalayan adventure the most unique experience I have had so far. What stands out is the strength and spirit of the Himalayan culture. While decked out in my state of the art mountain gear: hiking boots, trekking poles, and high-tech, dry wicking layers, a porter in nothing more*

167

*than flip-flops, cut off pants and a t-shirt would pass me carrying 75 plus pounds on his back. Women and sometimes children too, carry heavy loads of food, clothing, and various other necessities. Essentially, the things that we mindlessly purchase in a store are carried high up into that stunning and harsh mountain region on the backs of its inhabitants. Even the homes in which they live, and the lodges where we stayed were all carried up there board by board with great effort. I return to this inspiring image whenever I think that something is too difficult."*     —*Camille Attell*

Julie Hoppe is a friend of my sister Tina. She's an avid triathlete and a professional accountant.

*"This trip was a life changing adventure. I left for Nepal with my career in the air and all of my belongings in storage. I found great clarity up at the altitude of Base Camp. Upon returning I started a successful business and now feel happy and fulfilled."*     —*Julie Hoppe*

Caryn Kralovansky is a financial advisor and an avid cyclist. For Caryn, going to Base Camp was a "bucket list" item.

*"The overall experience and introduction to CAF was a reminder that nothing should be taken for granted. In 2009 I was told I had the hips of a 60 year old and would likely need a full hip replacement before I reached 50. It hit home how much I've taken for granted my ability to participate in athletics. Every day I work to prove that physical therapist wrong. Life doesn't always cooperate in helping us accomplish our dreams but with determination, courage and support from others we can still make those dreams happen."*     —*Caryn Kralovansky*

Branden Rubasky is a former airline pilot who is now a financial advisor in Redondo Beach, California. His wife and young daughter were supportive of him taking advantage of this opportunity for an adventure, and since his return they have added a new member to the family.

*"I am most proud of the groups' accomplishments over my own. It was physically challenging, but being so far away from my family for so long was the worst part. But the fact that the whole group raised so much money, all*

*made it to Kala Patthar and Base Camp, really made it worthwhile and makes me glad I was part of the group."* —Branden Rubasky

Nancy Wallace from Alberta, Canada is a project manager in the IT telecom business. We met her and her family while SCUBA diving in Belize and knew they were fun and adventurous.

*"Going up the hill helped me to find the best in myself. Coming down helped me to understand how to share it with the community around me. Being home, I hold new measures of work ethic, determination and community in my paradigm. Within a year I completed a certification that I had been putting off for a couple of years, which has led me to new career opportunities and provided an injection of confidence. Amazing how many small mountains I find to scale in my everyday life. I draw from my time on Everest and I plow back into my symbolic ice field."* —Nancy Wallace

Cory Markin is Nancy's partner and a general contractor/developer who enjoys the outdoors and is a SCUBA diving and motorbike enthusiast.

*"I was fortunate to have Nancy and Jaymen along with me to share this epic journey to Base Camp, while so many others left their families back at home. There were times on the trail when I needed motivation to keep hiking and they were there to keep me going. I came to realize on this trip that with the support of good friends and family, anything is possible."* —Cory Markin

At 17 years old, Nancy's son Jaymen Greenslade was by far the youngest member of the group. He is physically fit and added a youthful enthusiasm and energy to the crew.

*"I did not expect this experience to affect my every day life the way it has. I think I arrived in Nepal young and naïve, and left with such a larger appreciation of all that life has to offer. I gave one of the Sherpas my iPod Touch and use it to communicate with him to this day. I found peace on the trip, and it will always be a memory I share with my family."* —Jaymen Greenslade

We met Jeff Roberts while hiking Mt. Whitney, long before our Seven Summits quest began. He is a litigator and trial attorney with a wife and two kids back at home. Jeff is a high energy and highly entertaining individual who never hesitates to speak his mind.

*"It was time to step out of the box and experience something far from my comfort zone. By doing this trip I have developed a real appreciation for the slogan "Just do it." I want to fill my life with more diverse and new experiences. I am far more willing to try new things than before I went to Nepal, and appreciate the opportunity to expand my horizons and personal outlook in this way."*

*—Jeff Roberts*

Lou Alvarado is a fraternity brother and a commercial banker. Prior to the trip his workload had mounted due to a department closure and the trek was a great escape for him.

*"This opportunity was from my Creator. I realized I had my nose buried in my own pressures at work/home and the fund raising allowed me to use talents for others as manifested through the work CAF does. This is what makes life full and rich—not what we do for a living but what service we do for our fellow man. As a result of this experience I am pursuing a new career path to use my traditional banking skills and experience in the venue of micro-finance. I want to help the small business entrepreneurs in poor/developing countries escape from poverty and contribute positively to society."*

*—Lou Alvarado*

Fritz Wickman runs his family-owned structural steel engineering business. He is a fraternity brother of mine and towering above all of the locals at 6'7" tall, he was a commanding presence on the mountain.

*"Our trip to the Himalaya and Everest Base Camp was unique. It changed me. Unlike my other experiences, the trek was an introspective journey to altitude, an approach like no other. During this time I shed the responsibilities and obligations I built-up around me in the business I left far behind. Even with the periodic opportunities for an Internet connection the journey became a process of 'unplugging' from the hustle and bustle of the life we've become accustomed to. I found myself in my element; altitude and natural beauty first introduced to me by my father as a child growing*

*up in the Alps. Places like the Tengboche Monastery and the Rhododendron Forest around it were magical and surreal."* —*Fritz Wickman*

BJ Wahl is another fraternity brother of mine and is also in software development along with Rod. He is the father of four, which in itself is a lofty challenge.

*"The experience made me realize that regardless of what you do, if you do it with great people it will take any trip from an incredible experience to an truly epic adventure! I look forward to reliving the trip with all 22 of my new best friends in the many years to come. Seeing the passion that Paul and Denise showed in setting an incredibly lofty goal and ultimately achieving it, while also working to help support a great organization like CAF has really motivated me. I have started working with a volunteer organization Engineers Without Borders to help make a difference in the lives of people who haven't had the opportunities we have had in life. In the years to come I hope to do even more and be a part of making truly significant changes in the world."* —*BJ Wahl*

Edgars Gulbis is an entrepreneur in finance and is originally from Latvia.

*"It was a phenomenal experience. Probably one of the hardest things I have ever done, however, the exposure to culture, people, and environment was priceless. After standing at 18,500 feet and looking at the Khumbu Icefall, I had only one thing to say to those who want to go higher—either you are crazy about mountains, or just crazy. I am going back."* —*Edgars Gulbis*

Rounding out the group is Dace Sprukte, a financial analyst, also from Latvia, and Edgars' wife.

*"Nepal taught me to appreciate the simple things in life and cherish every step I take towards my goals in life."* —*Dace Sprukte*

From the bottom of our hearts, we sincerely thank this spectacular group of individuals, our friends—for the experience of a lifetime. You have all made an Impact on us and so many others—you have reached your S.U.M.M.I.T.!

# ACKNOWLEDGEMENTS

In many ways, Step #12—Build Quality Relationships, is the most important of all the Steps to the Summit. Without the wonderful people with whom I have shared productive and rewarding relationships, this book would simply not be possible. I have also discovered that writing a book can be more difficult, require more determination and discipline (Step #4), more faith (Step #8), and more focus (Step #11) than climbing a mountain. Therefore I would like to thank all of those who helped make *Steps to the Summit* a reality, as well as those who helped create the many triumphs described on its pages.

First and foremost to my wife Denise, who was with me every step of the way during all of the adventures, including the book writing adventure. Her vivid recollection of events, detailed journal, and continuous review of the chapters made it a better book.

To my family, especially to my mom Stela for encouraging me to never give up (Step #15) and for making me a better person.

To the entire CAF staff in particular Jennifer Rose and Virginia Tinley for coordinating and supporting our fundraising efforts. And to all of the challenged athletes who live courageously (Step #2) every day with a special thanks to "One-Arm Willie" Stewart, Scout Bassett, Sarah Reinertsen, and John Siciliano for providing inspiration to me in their own unique ways.

To my good friend Cindy Bertram for helping me write this book. Being just a satellite phone call away as our communications coordinator for two months while on Everest, made it feel like we climbed the mountain together. Writing *Steps to the Summit* together was a tremendous undertaking, and I don't think I could have selected a better co-author.

To my friends and business colleagues who reviewed the book line by line, providing valuable feedback, and each offering unique suggestions which ultimately made for a better book: Bob Kurkjian, John Barnhill, Dave Jochim, Fred Jager, Stela Fejtek, Judy Smith, Alan Shanken, Paul Whisenand, and Chris Gayde.

Also to professional editors India Penney and Leslie Tilley who further refined the final product, as well as to author Robert Liljenwall for his early collaboration on the content. To Amy Cole of JPL Design Solutions for her skillful work on the cover and interior layout, and to Karen Allen for her graphic design work.

To all of my clients over the years who shared their insights with me into their business success. And to Fred Jager and Ken Kaiser for stepping in to help me manage the sale transactions for some of these same clients, while I found myself high up on a mountain somewhere around the globe.

To our Everest guides Scott Woolums and Bill Allen of Mountain Trip for always keeping us safe, to our climbing team of Ania Lichota, Vivian Rigney, and Cindy Abbott for always keeping it interesting, and to our entire Sherpa team for always working so hard and being genuinely happy to do anything for us: Dawa Gyaljen Sherpa, Da Ongchhu Sherpa, Temba Sherpa, Karma Gyaljen Sherpa, Passang Tendi Sherpa, Tarke Sherpa, Passang Gomba Sherpa, Sonam Chhiring Sherpa, Sange Sherpa, Pem Chhiri Sherpa, Pem Chhotar Sherpa, Da Kusang Sherpa, Perba Surki Sherpa, Mingma Lapka Sherpa, Da Phinju Sherpa, Mindu Sherpa, and Ongdi Sherpa.

To our Everybody to Everest team for all you have done for us and for CAF, and also for sharing your reflections about how the experience impacted your lives. Also thank you to those who truly wanted to participate but were unable to make the journey. ...this time.

To Stephen Somer and Collett Kreizenbeck for introducing us to Lindsay Grubb and Jenna Wolfe at the Today Show. Thank you for your interest in airing our story and to Daisy Lin, Dr. Bruce Hensel, Chuck Henry, and Colleen Williams at NBC News as well, for helping to spread the word about an important cause we are so passionate about.

To the following companies for generously donating gear put to use as fundraising incentives and raffle/auction items: Sport Chalet, Outdoor Research, REI, Marmot, and GoPro.

In closing, an enormous thank you to all of our friends and family who supported us with great interest over the years as we climbed the Seven Summits, and who generously contributed to CAF along the way. Each and every one of you holds a special place in our hearts and minds and we will be forever grateful for your generosity and for your friendship.

*The Everest Summit Banner bearing names of our*
*larger donors to CAF who helped "carry us" to the top.*

If I have somehow neglected to mention any names, please know this is an oversight. ...Or perhaps a temporary memory lapse due to my exposure to oxygen-devoid high altitudes! I do wish to express my gratitude to everybody (whether specifically mentioned by name or not) who has contributed positively in some way to the life Denise and I share together. These are things we will not forget, and we appreciate you tremendously for them.

Finally to you for purchasing this book and recommending it to friends, you are making an impact in the lives of grateful challenged athletes, as 100% of the profits go directly to CAF.

*To purchase additional copies of "Steps to the Summit" as gifts for others, or to get the enhanced eBook version complete with exciting videos to enjoy on your iPad, Kindle, Nook or other tablet device, please visit:*
**http://StepsToTheSummit.com**

*For inquiries about booking Paul and Denise Fejtek as guest speakers for corporate and professional events, please visit the Media & Speaking page at the above web address or email:*
**info@stepstothesummit.com**

*To learn more about advisory services provided by Hunter Wise Financial Group please visit:* **www.hunterwise.com** *or contact:* **pfejtek@hunterwise.com**

MT. MCKINLEY
20,320 FEET
JUNE 2007

E

NORTH
AMERICA

AF

SOUTH
AMERICA

MT. ACONCAGUA
22,841 FEET
JAN. 2005

VINSON MASSIF
16,067 FEET
DEC. 2009